C0-ARS-248

WHICH WAY RELIGION?

By
HARRY F. WARD

WHICH WAY RELIGION?

BY

HARRY F. WARD

*Professor of Christian Ethics in Union
Theological Seminary*

GEN. THEO. SEMINARY
LIBRARY
NEW YORK

NEW YORK
THE MACMILLAN COMPANY
1931

261.1T
W212
90966

Copyright, 1931,
By HARRY F. WARD.

All rights reserved—no part of this book
may be reproduced in any form without
permission in writing from the publisher.

Set up and electrotyped.

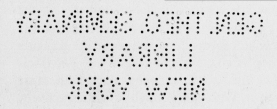

GEN. THEO. SEMINARY
LIBRARY
NEW YORK

SET UP BY BROWN BROTHERS LINOTYPERS
PRINTED IN THE UNITED STATES OF AMERICA
BY THE FERRIS PRINTING COMPANY

PREFACE

AFTER the manner of other days, this brief writing might properly be called *A Tract for the Times*. That indeed is all it is—a tract—addressed first to those who have any responsibility in office or membership for the course of our religious agencies and beyond them to any who have a concern for the future of religion. These persons will write into history the answer to the question it raises.

Of those who will naturally resent judgments expressed in the analysis of current events and forces I would request that disregarding these, they attend to the main challenge of the book and find for themselves a working relation between the things of time and the forces that are timeless.

I have assumed that readers will be familiar with the phrase *The Acquisitive Society*. If any have not met it, I would urge them to read the brief volume under that title by R. H. Tawney. Two other terms that I use, *The Great Society* and *The Beloved Community*, have been made familiar by Graham Wallas and Josiah Royce respectively. But those who are familiar with the writings of these authors will perceive that I use the terms in a wider sense than they do.

The reason that I have made summary statements about our present economic arrangements without supporting evidence is that I have recently discussed that subject at some length in *Our Economic Morality*. Because some comments on that book revealed a misunderstanding of my view of the relation of the ethic of Jesus to the modern world, I have this time, at the cost of some slight repetition, taken the space to make my position on that matter sufficiently clear.

At first glance the use of the word religion to cover a discussion mainly concerned with American Protestantism may seem unwarranted. But, as I trust becomes plain before the discussion ends, what happens to the Protestant churches of this country has considerable significance for the future of religion in general.

The sketchy description of the religious aspects of Communism in the last chapter records convictions developed in the course of a long acquaintance with the Socialist movement and crystallized during a visit to Russia in 1924. They have therefore been confirmed, not suggested, by recent similar and more detailed expressions from other writers.

It remains to be said that the topics herein treated were discussed verbally in October, 1928 before the Rock River Conference of the Methodist Episcopal Church at the invitation of its Board of Ministerial Training; again in June, 1929 before the Summer Conference of Ministers at Union Theological Seminary; and again in July of that year, with other matters, before the Conference of Student Secretaries of the Young Men's Christian Association at Estes Park, Colorado. These several discussions constituted a development rather than a repetition. This is still more true of the process of putting their essential features into written form.

Lonely Lake, Ontario   HARRY F. WARD.
September, 1930

CONTENTS

[7]

WHICH WAY RELIGION?

CHAPTER I

THE CHOICE BEFORE US

1. THE DEMAND FOR SUBMISSION

AMONG the people called Christians the enemies of religious living are traditionally identified as the world, the flesh, and the devil. It is a convenient list, and accurate enough. Also it has plenty of support elsewhere. Under whatever name or form man follows the quest of the holy he finds himself opposed by forces whose works are evil, by the appetites of his body, by the pomp and power of the organized ways of society. Against these foes all religions have issued their defiance and organized their assault. From them they have all, at times, fled in fear; and with them, at other times, have made truce and even alliance.

The Christian religion in its day has feared, exorcised, served, and disbelieved the devil. It has renounced, repressed, ignored, and blessed the lusts of the flesh. It has defied, ruled, imitated, and sought to transform the world. Each of these differing and contradictory things it may be seen doing somewhere at the present moment. Some sections of the Protestant denominations are now learning what man may do with the flesh and ought to do with the devil. The human sciences have thrown a flood of light upon the generation and development of evil which en-

[11]

ables theology to come to closer grips with one of its toughest problems and practical religion to attempt more accurately to guide the steps of erring mortals. From the same source there is coming the groundwork of a technic for the control of bodily appetites in the interest of the highest ideals of social living. But the world, with its principalities and powers, its spiritual wickedness in high places! Who knows what to do with that? Science is just as much tied in with it as religion and shows no greater capacity for being disinterested.

When the world is not confused with the flesh by asceticism, it is set down in our traditional religious writings as the temporal or the secular order. The former phrase contrasts it with the domain of the spirit, the latter with the dominion of the church. In both aspects its claims are asserted and established through the state. In the modern world the authority of the state is increasingly the authority of the immediate, practical, sectional interests of life against that of its larger, longer, intangible aspects, whether they be voiced by religion or science. So the question of whether religion is to transform or conform to the world comes to a focus at the point of its relation to the state. Are the churches any more sure of what this is finally to be in the United States than they are in Italy or Russia?

The issue is complicated by the fact that to-day the state is more than government. Increasingly it absorbs the control of economic organization and the direction of social well-being. It is apparent that politics and economics have become indissolubly joined by machine production and social planning. These trends are revealing to American Protestantism the limitations of its doctrine of separation of church and state and of its inherited position that economic morality, like peace with God, is under the sole sovereignty of the individual conscience and without corporate control. That these principles of isolation and neutrality are unworkable is made abundantly clear by the activities of the American churches in the matters of prohibition and war, and by their utterances concerning the industrial problem and other social questions which are also matters of state policy.

In its view of the relation of religion to the organized world the negative aspect of Protestantism has dominated. For the most part it has been content with denying the position and claims of Romanism. It has refused to follow the imperialists of Rome in their assertion of temporal sovereignty and its saints in their abandonment of the world as evil. Through most of its history it has maintained in theory and practice that the corporate life would automatically become Christianized through the activities and influence of individual Christians. In these latter days there has arisen considerable demand for a conscious attempt to transform the world in the direction of the religious ideal and, without a wide understanding of what was involved, there has developed in response to particular pressing needs a substantial program in this direction. These activities put organized religion into further dependence upon the agencies and resources of the world and thus increase the tendency of ecclesiasticism to support the present as the best of all possible orders.

Manifestly the course of events insistently thrusts into the consciousness of the churches the question of their relation to that network of practical arrangements in which man both attempts and denies the visions of the spirit.

Once again the quest for such unity as is possible in the diversity of human existence is calling the heirs of that disorganized world which was broken apart by the Renaissance and the Reformation to discover what is the right relationship between the chief institutions of corporate living—religion, government, economics. Which of them is to set the moral tone and quality for life? If all of them together, then in what proportion and relative position?

The question becomes clamorous at the point of the practical relations between church and state. Protestantism, despite its official neutrality, is by now deeply involved in the political-economic order that is the real government. To both its aspects it has given moral sanctions; from both it has accepted substantial benefits. It has put God behind the state and given divine approval to the economic virtues. From the latter it has derived its endowments and from the former their legal protection. Of necessity there are resultant obligations and the reckoning is now being called for. From various quarters in various ways is now heard the demand that organized religion and the religious conscience subordinate themselves to the state and to the interests which the state for the moment represents.

This demand for the submission of religion to the purposes of the state emerges from our experience in the days of the World War. When this nation belatedly entered the conflict, the government assumed, and the citizens took it for granted, that the churches would aid in the undertaking. Here, where separation of church and state is proclaimed, the churches became just as much an arm of the government as they did in those countries that have a state church. If national officials had not laid out a program which specifically included the activities of religious organizations, if the leaders of those bodies had not hastened to offer their services, their local members would have accomplished the same result by using their church affiliations in furtherance of that part of the war plan for which they were responsible; just as now through military and patriotic organizations some of them demand that the national flag occupy the chief place in buildings dedicated to world brotherhood. This sort of thing was and is just as inevitable—perhaps more so—when religion is viewed as one aspect of a democratic society as when it is the buttress of an autocratic order.

In support of the national purpose and plan in the war religious agencies contributed more than endurance for its sufferings and consolation for its bereavements. They also stimulated the fighting spirit. Religion was not as consciously used for release or stimulus as were nicotine by all, and alcohol and brothels by some belligerents. But the question is whether in the outcome its function was essentially different. The utterances of some excitable preachers who both forgot and denied Jesus can be dismissed from the reckoning. The real thing that religion in this country did to support the war was to interpret it in terms of universal values. In this it was led by a president who was a very powerful preacher. It is now apparent that the function of those who occupied less resounding pulpits was to help other publicity agencies cloak the national interests of the allied and associated powers in the garb of freedom and justice for all mankind. This was essential if our entrance into the war was to gather popular enthusiasm behind it. A nation founded in rebellion against the imperial state, taught to regard it as anathema

[15]

and drilled in isolation from its policies, cannot change position without self-deception. It must make its war, as it must develop its imperialism, for the benefit of others.

Here was where organized religion played its chief rôle. For the most part it had outgrown the tribal god. In large degree it was too enlightened to divide the deity against himself by making him merely a nationalist protector. Yet in a time of confusion, when the needs of the common people everywhere were struggling with the secret purposes and plans of the privileged and powerful, religion in this country weighted the scale. It put behind our participation in the war the final moral authority—the only authority that its founder allows to God—that of universal ethical values. It asked men to fight, and it helped them to fight, for world brotherhood. Thus it came about that the submission of the churches to the state was practically complete. They exercised no peculiar function. They offered no effective criticism. Despite their early declaration they did not even defend the rights of their own conscientious objectors. They were unable to carry through their own gesture of attempting reconciliation by way of leaders of the same religion on both sides of the battle line. They did not understand that when he makes war, man as citizen of the state obliterates man as member of humanity; immediate, sectional interests transcend those larger, longer concerns and possibilities which are the particular province of religion.

Thus when peace came as suddenly as war had come, organized religion, like the statesman whose preacher voice it had followed, found itself utterly unable to secure the aims for which it had sent men like sheep to the slaughter. The reason is now plain. The revelation of the secret agreements and real purposes of the allies, the later publication of the documents concerning the origins of the conflict, and finally the writings of the official propagandists laying bare their technic, make it plain that religion was used to deceive the American people, just as in Germany it supported "the myth of encirclement" by which a recent volume of one of her historians shows that nation was duped. That its leaders were themselves deceived and played their part unwittingly does not lessen the consequences. The unconscious use of the final moral authority for ends now seen to be contrary to its nature left it so weakened that it could not serve the desperate need of those whose energies had been exhausted by the war, for whom the imperative of the death grapple had destroyed all other sanctions. Official religion had no tonic for a generation that was left by the war without enough moral vigor to pass a child labor law, without sufficient capacity for moral indignation to rebuke unparalleled political corruption or charity enough to refrain from taking our pound of flesh from suffering creditors. The moral debility that always follows a serious war was this time increased and prolonged by the consciousness of misdirected spiritual energy. If any ethical reality in our religion survived the blasphemy of the trenches, it then had to endure the revelation that what its guardians had been doing was to mistake another golden calf for the great God.

A speedy result of this transfer of moral authority was that immediately after the war the churches were faced with a demand from certain forces of the business world for submission similar to that which had been accorded the state. For a decade before the war church bodies had occasionally uttered judgment concerning inhuman and unjust industrial conditions. When this was done with much thoroughness in the report on the steel strike of 1919 by the Commission of Inquiry of the Interchurch World Movement, it was followed by propaganda from industrial agencies urging business men to cut off their subscriptions to any religious agencies that continued to meddle with industrial matters. This effort was soon accompanied by an organized attempt to intimidate or secure the dismissal of teachers and preachers who had criticized the state or industry or the militarists and money-makers who identified themselves with those institutions. Neither of these demands was supported by the more intelligent leaders of politics or business and the visible results were few.

Out of them however there developed quite a formi-dable blacklist movement carried on by an alliance of industrial, military, and patriotic organizations. The in-dustrialist propagandists provided from their files what passed for data from which the militaristic patriots, espe-cially those of the gentler sex, prepared lists of speakers who ought not to be heard and sometimes not even al-lowed to speak by good citizens, and of organizations which ought not to be supported. By the end of the decade this blacklist movement managed to make itself ridiculous by its misinformation, and by including quite conservative religious leaders and agencies because they had said or done something that could be construed as contrary to the views and interests of some of the black-listers. Also, a few suits for libel dampened the zeal of its promoters.

It would be shortsighted however to dismiss these crude attempts to starve and bludgeon the critical function of religion into silence as either temporary or insignificant. The effort to stop religion from expressing moral judgment concerning policies of state and of the powerful economic interests that manage a good deal of the time to use the state for their advantage is continuous and in the nature of the case must be so. As fast as existing repressive propagandist agencies are discredited new ones appear, operating in more subtle form. At the present moment a new drive against the "Reds" is being organized in Congress, to extend to educational institutions. These efforts have a significance far beyond their meager concrete achievements. In so far as they are directed against religious leaders and agencies, they register a new consciousness in certain circles concerning the possibilities of organized religion. They are the anticipatory strains of a demand which will become continuously more imperious, because it expresses the nature of the forces upon which the modern state rests.

When the propaganda of those who are now so crudely voicing this demand that religion be subordinate to the alleged interests of the nationalistic state is examined, two things at once strike the eye. The union between militarists and industrialists is so close that it is impossible to tell where one interest begins and the other leaves off. These joint forces identify themselves with the state. Both these mergers are a natural result of our present National Defense Act with its provision for a large body of reserve officers added to our habit of using government to help business. Thus many are led to acquire a sense of public authority and service in the pursuit of their own welfare. To such persons radicals, and even reformers, who are anathema to certain business interests are thereby and therefore unpatriotic. Likewise, those opposed to war or even to large military and naval establishments are thereby and therefore Bolsheviks. This is a perfectly natural position for patriots in a state whose chief concern is property and whose main reliance is force.

If the United States is not yet there, how fast we move in that direction is to be seen in the recent decisions of our final authority, the Supreme Court, concerning dissenters from the prevailing policies and philosophy of government. Here, and not in the hysteria of the blacklisters, is recorded the vitality of that claim of moral supremacy for the state which was asserted in war time; here is revealed also the power of the economic forces that lie behind that claim. The final claim of absolute moral authority for the state is set forth in a decision refusing citizenship to an alien, a woman past fifty years of age, whose humanitarian conscience would not permit her to promise to bear arms in defense of the country. In addition, because she had under cross-questioning avowed a certain "cosmic consciousness," the decision affirmed that she did not possess a sufficiently vigorous nationalism to make a good citizen. Under the stimulus or shelter of this decision the lower courts have gone further and further in refusing naturalization to aliens who, on religious grounds, are not willing to fight with weapons of destruction. A distinguished professor of theology is refused because, with no religious objection to war in general, he will not serve in a conflict which his conscience, directed by God, does not approve. Three women, one after another—a British Quakeress, a German Mennonite and a former and future war nurse—are all rejected because their religion leads them to conclude that war is wrong. Finally, a Methodist minister who has no religious objection to fighting is refused because he will not specifically promise to take part in a hypothetical war of unprovoked aggression.

These decisions it must be remembered are made by courts which are constantly identifying property with the state, business interests with public welfare, and preferring the claim to dividends to the right of civil liberties. Thus for a state which is increasingly a limited holding corporation we have written into the law the claim of omnipotence and infallibility that has been taken away from the church, and which a growing section of mankind is unable to allow to God. If these decisions stand and the churches are without courage to contest them and power to get them reversed, then the outcome of the separation of church and state is the subjection of religion to the state. Once again the god of the nation is set up in place of the god of mankind whom our religion has been seeking to establish. This time Mammon is his name. And what a god! Without even the virtues that did something to redeem the brutality of Mars.

2. TOLERANCE AND ITS CONSEQUENCES

The opportunity for American Protestantism to clearly see and sharply meet this issue is diminished by the fact that it arises within the churches and not simply between the churches and the state or the churches and the dominant economic forces. The question of whether economic nationalism is to have moral supremacy over a religion of world fellowship, whether the state or the living God of all mankind is to be served, runs a line of cleavage within the churches, through the clergy as well as between clergy and laity. Some of the men who voice the demand of organized militarists and industrialists for the silencing of moral criticism of their policies are within the churches. If that demand is to be enforced with the starvation of persons and institutions it must secure sufficient support from within. A war carried on solely from without could not win. It would only strengthen the forces it was seeking to destroy.

Within the churches there has been in the decade since the war a marked growth of moral judgment concerning war and militarism. This is a reaction from the war time submission of religion to the state. But there has been no corresponding growth of moral criticism of the economic order in whose soil are embedded the roots of war, militarism, the new nationalism and imperialism. The utterances of religious bodies on industrial and economic issues do not show the same sharpness that was evident before the war. There is a preference for informational statements without a clear expression of moral judgment. There has been no successor to the steel strike report, though occasions have not been lacking.

Several reasons for this difference from the decade before the war may be set down. There is the absorption of the moral energy of one section of the church forces in the movement against war and of another section in the prohibition situation. There is the inhibiting fact that part of the financial gains of the period have been incorporated into expensive church building projects. Unquestionably also the vociferous antics of the blacklisters have occasioned some subconscious self-expression within the forces of religion. Then there is the paradoxical situation that the growth of tolerance in the churches has resulted in a limitation of the field for moral judgment. This tolerance of pew for pulpit, of disagreeing laymen for the statements of church bodies, is related to the general growth of intellectual liberalism with its willingness to hear both sides, and its fondness for discussion without either moral judgment or action. Where this attitude dominates the contact of religion with the economic order, the situation is pleasingly frictionless.

Then there appears a further tendency to maintain harmony by a division of function which limits the utterances of the pulpit and of church bodies to general principles and leaves details to the laymen. In certain cases, particularly where the preacher is held in great affection, or where there is a group of laymen unusually desirous of discovering the ethical implications of their religion, this tolerance has no limitation; it extends to the concrete. These situations are not many, and few of them have stood up against the strain of a bitter strike, as few withstood the worse tension of war days. It is the same with denominational or federated statements. As long, for example, as they confine themselves to asserting that Christian principles should be applied to the acquisition and use of property, nobody objects. But when they attempt to decide what forms of property are not justified by the ethics of the gospel, then the war is on.

This attitude of tolerance, even when limited to general principles, is a clear advance from the position that the pulpit does not and cannot know enough concerning matters of state or business to talk about them, and in any event should not meddle with what is beyond its concern. But if we stop there, what happens? Generalities sufficiently repeated inevitably become platitudes. And platitudes in the moral realm are deadly. Those who continue to listen to them become as gospel hardened as those who formerly had their religious sensibilities atrophied by the repeated appeals of an unreal emotional evangelism. If the ethics of the gospel whose rediscovery is the distinctive achievement of the modern Protestant spirit are to be so used that presently, like the creeds and the liturgies, they evoke from the majority of communicants only a stereotyped intellectual assent and an emotional reaction which has no results in life, then Protestanism will have lost its opportunity to become a vital religion. Hearing and understanding, without doing the words of Jesus, it will have built its house upon the sands.

If the separation of function between minister and laymen which assigns general principles to one and concrete matters to the other could become a real division of labor, a genuine collaboration in a common effort to transform the world, something would be gained. But, for most laymen, behind the concession that it is the business of the pulpit to proclaim the ethical principles that should be worked out in the whole of life is the reservation, expressed or implied, that these principles after all are an impossible ideal—as indeed they are in a world that relies upon acquisitiveness to motivate and force to conserve it. As long as this is true and the efforts of pulpit and pew are not jointly directed toward changing it, the sermons and the statements that expound the principles of Jesus move in one direction, the weekday activities in another. But if the laymen are led to understand by concrete criticism of current life how much of it has to be changed if their religion is to live and grow, then they may also see the necessity for working out in the churches

—for a very different purpose—a similar collaboration on the moral problem of civilization to that which has been realized in the universities on its technical aspects between scientists and leaders of business.

If the achievement of tolerance between clergy and laity is to leave us in that state of balance between conflicting forces so dear to the liberal mind, the result will be a much more effective direction of the course of religion by the joint forces of the state and the economic order than could ever be achieved by the crude bludgeoning of our Black Hundreds. When preachers proclaim and congregations applaud, when national religious gatherings adopt and newspapers print, general principles that are revolutionary in their implications, the impression is spread that something serious is being done. Whereas, if there is no actual grappling with existing institutions, the most important consequence of preaching and pronouncements is that the edge of the gospel is blunted and its capacity for transforming civilization impaired. That job is then left to the Communists, and society is without any process for critical revaluation and reconstruction.

It is then a joint demand that the churches of this country now face—from without that the voice of religion concerning certain matters be silenced and from within that it be circumscribed. This demand asks us to develop the other worldly strain in our religion, to ignore the fact that man must live in two worlds at the same time, and to evade the difficulty of discovering how this may satisfactorily be done. But history makes it plain that whenever the church ceases attempting to transform this world it becomes conformed to it. The days of the high priests and Pharisees, of the corrupt period of the Papacy and of eighteenth century Protestantism are sufficient cases in point. Religion is both a changing and a conserving force. It can maintain its vitality only by performing both functions. When it stops changing society it conserves only the forces of decay and so becomes the source of corruption. When it runs away from the problem of change it does not escape the world, but comes into deeper bondage to it. When religion is not used to change the present order, its communal function is to throw its powerful sanctions around existing institutions. So to-day economic imperialism masquerades as benevolence to weaker nations and selfish profit-seeking as service. As in the war, self-interest seizes the universal values of religion to cloak its purposes.

The question here is bigger than the issue between church and state. Protestantism claims nothing but a moral authority and that not for its institutions but for the ethic of Jesus as the developing morality of mankind struggling toward a democratic society. However imperfectly it has developed them, the logic of its position and its historic tendencies are toward the discovery of universal ethical standards. On the other hand, the state, as it exists to-day, is sectional and separating. It speaks and acts without its borders for a part of mankind against the rest. Within its boundaries it is most of the time the voice and arm of the economically powerful group. It is these two voices that are speaking in the blacklists and in the decision of the Supreme Court that one who refuses to kill on command cannot be a citizen. Something else speaks in the outlawry of war as an instrument of national policy, as it spoke in the old equalitarian ideals of this land only to be denied by both our concentration of wealth and our economic imperialism. If the churches then yield to the authority of this nationalistic state, this local economic society, they are yielding the interests of the whole to the desire of a part. So doing, they betray mankind and God again, as they did in the war, by throwing the sanction of an ethical religion around the lesser groupings of mankind to the destruction of that larger fellowship which is their aim.

In this issue it is the function of religion in modern society which is at stake. What happens to its institutions is of lesser importance. Since the Geneva and New England attempts turned out otherwise than their founders planned, Protestantism has lacked any theory of the place of religion in the community, of its relation to the other institutions of society. Rome knows where it wants to stand. Protestantism does not—yet. In Europe, as state churches, it has been the bulwark of established authority. Here its theoretical relationship to the powers that be has been one of indirect influence through individual character. Recently through minority movements in Europe and in this country, also here through some general undertakings, it has been trying to advance in another direction, endeavoring to infuse the world with the vital principles of Jesus, seeking thus to transform continuously human institutions as well as persons in the direction of their highest possibilities. While in theology it has been talking about an immanent God, in practice it has been developing an immanent religion, whose authority is to be exerted not through potentates of either church or state but through ethical results in men and institutions.

Now that attempt is sharply challenged by powerful interests whose nature drives them to establish once more, if they can, the omnipotent state, to mold an empire even under the slogan of democracy. Whether it be here or in Russia, those who need an absolute state to execute their designs find their real enemy to be not an infallible or superstitious church, but an ethical religion which is as antithetical to absolutism as it is to infallibility and superstition. It is not to the credit of our intellectuals that so many of them have been diverted to a fight that has passed the point of decision—between the scientific spirit and an obscurantist religion—while the major battle between the immoral state and an ethical religion was in the making. It is in this struggle between the state as a self-conscious, self-seeking economic organization and the larger, longer interests of man represented by a developing ethical religion that the question of the final moral authority for human society is to be worked out.

It was historically as inevitable as it will be significant that the clash between the tendencies in Protestantism toward an ethical religion and the interests that control the acquisitive society should come to a head in this country. In England and Germany Protestantism inherited a relation to the state, and therefore, grew naturally into a place in the empires created by commercialism and industrialism, meanwhile here it was more perfectly and purely a religious individualism. As such it was taking part in establishing a new society, which was to be different. Now the scene is changed. America has become wealthy and powerful and the democratic experiment comes to be regarded with doubt and distrust. A newer attempt at organizing the life of man challenges its accomplishments and awakes its fears. It moves into the position of defense so long occupied by European states. It seeks security for its wealth and its constitution. Hence, American religion is called on for the first time to come to the defense of an established order. For all its abandonment of the economic problem, for all its determination to leave the state alone, American Protestantism has now to make up its mind concerning its relation toward the society made by the industrial revolution.

New as it is for American Protestantism, the situation in which it now finds itself is not new in the history of our religion. What the blacklisters, the Supreme Court, and the new capitalism is offering to organized religion has been met before. They offer to preachers of the gospel of Jesus the power and the glory of this world—the prestige of being the honored and influential ministers of rich churches in a mighty state. The price is not that they shall fall down and worship the old god of force and greed but that they shall help to keep him disguised in his modern mask of benevolence and service. Once before in its early organized days the Christian religion met such a choice unaware. Then it consented to become the official religion of the Roman Empire, whose ways of force and later its ways of wealth it consequently ceased to challenge. After that imperial Christianity ceased to be the religion of Jesus, whose manner of life was carried forward by minority movements within the churches. These were either repressed or in their turn became prosperous and conformed to the ways of the world. Now American Protestantism, free from limiting historic entanglements with a powerful state, must decide its destiny. Will it become the beneficiary, then the servant, and finally the coadjutor of a greater empire than Rome? Or will it challenge man to a different way of life than the pursuit of wealth and power?

3. SHIFTING CURRENTS

This question is raised by developments within the world of organized religion as well as by demands from without. It is no accident that while the issue of the relation of religious institutions to the state and the economic order has been raised by current events, at the same time the question of the nature of religion has been projected by its exponents. The choice of accepting or rejecting the demand of the acquisitive society for submission is also a choice concerning what kind of religion we will have. On that, too, Protestantism has never had occasion to make up its mind. Because it was a protest movement, and that only against certain aspects of Rome, it has been feeling in various directions, moving now backward, now forward, never certain of the main line of its development.

In the decade since the war, there has been a marked shift in the currents of religion. Naturally enough the emotional upheaval occasioned by our entrance into the war and the way we fought it found a later expression in the growth of various emotional religious cults with the apocalyptic emphasis. Just as natural a consequence of our sudden stimulation of hate was the intensifying of pious belligerency among our religious illiterates. Militant fundamentalism and antievolution laws were inevitable. They were only an expansion of existing tendencies. More significant was the shift of emphasis in liberal religious circles. There interest was diverted from the ethical problem to the mystery of the cosmos, to the beautifying of public worship, and to the psychology of the inner life.

In the twenty years before the great conflict two new movements appeared in the religious life of this country. One which began with the name social service is now commonly known as the social gospel, the term being a revelation of the unnatural division in our modern, individualistic Christianity between the life of the person and that of the group. The other still carries its birth name—religious education. It is perhaps more characteristically American than the social movement in religion which has about the same expression in Great Britain as here. The two developments have much in common, both as to origin and objective. They register differently the effect of the scientific movement upon religion—one getting its stimulus from the educational world, the other from the activities of philanthropy, social reform, and labor. They both look forward to changing human nature and the forms of its living. They are also mutually interdependent; neither can have any real achievement apart from the other. Without education which seeks that goal, the religious hope of achieving the Beloved Community is vain. Unless it is definitely directed to the changing of the life of man in all its expressions, religious education is but another academic exercise.

By the time the war broke the social service movement in the churches had become to a considerable extent institutionalized into stereotyped forms of activity, and the religious education movement showed signs of being absorbed in technic. Without the disillusionment of our futile attempt to make the world safe for democracy, the tough resistance of the acquisitive society to the transforming power of an ethical religion would have inclined many who sought that end to paths where there were more primroses and fewer thorns. The war, with its tremendous draft upon moral idealism and its additional evidence of the enormous difficulty of achieving the religious hope for human society, powerfully increased this tendency.

The hopes and plans for a peaceful progress into a new world had been destroyed. For some ministers this produced an attack upon war, for others an interest in psychiatry, for others a turning from the works of man to the ways of God, and for still others an absorption in liturgies, antiphonals and processionals. For a similar reason the theology of crisis spreads in Europe. In each hemisphere, in ways determined by the background, many ministers of religion exchanged preoccupation with the struggle of humanity for contemplation of the eternal mystery. In each the efforts of man were belittled. There it is said that man can do nothing for himself, here it is proclaimed by those for whom it once provided a way to catch the popular ear that the social gospel was a shallow, transient movement, that the real essence of religion lies elsewhere. In similar vein it is the habit of some European theologians to describe the social movement in religion as a typical American product, to dismiss it as mere activism, an expression of our excess energy, of our tendency to keep busy attending to the affairs of others.

Neither the critics of the so-called social gospel abroad nor its deserters at home, however, have touched the roots of the matter. That they lie too deep to be cut by the plowing of the war is evident from the fact that there is at present a revival of interest in the social meaning of Christianity. Important books on that question are appearing for the first time in nine years. Also there arises an aggressive religious Humanism. These developments express both the spirit of our times and the social nature of religion. Inevitably, since religion is an aspect of the total life of man, it must in any period be adapted to and colored by the whole set of social institutions with which it is intertwined, which also if it is vital it modifies in turn. Hence, the movement to develop religion in social living is part of the collectivism of the modern world, which inevitably increases under the compulsion of the machine and the impetus of science. This movement appears in the Orient as well as in the West, partly under the stimulus and example of Christian missions, partly also as a response to the needs created by industrialism, and through the contagion of the secular humanitarian movement. In all this interchange an ethical religion appears above the horizon, even as it did in the days of the eighth century prophets in Israel, but this time on a world scale.

Thus the social gospel movement is more than an expansion of religious activity. It raises once again the question of the nature of religion, asks what is its essence and purpose. Is it social product or revelation? Primarily intellectual, emotional, or ethical? For this world or the next? To uphold the existing order or to impel change? To buttress the prerogatives of the privileged and the authority of the powerful or to inspire and encourage the oppressed? To maintain yesterday, support to-day, or make to-morrow? If all of these, then in what order and proportion?

It appears then that American Protestantism has two choices simultaneously before it, one thrust from without and one arising within, one compelling us to take a position in relation to the political-economic order, the other calling us to decide what kind of religion we want. Both of these demands express underlying forces. The first voices the mechanistic and imperial nature of the industrial state, the second expresses the ethical character and ancestry of our religion. These historic forces now join in conflict, and the two choices offer us only one decision. To submit to the state is to reject an ethical religion. To defy the political-economic order is to choose the ethical imperative. If the nature of capitalistic industrialism had become as clear as did that of slavery, the choice would be consciously made. But because of the complexity of industrial society, the issue is likely to be decided subconsciously by the preference for a certain aspect of the religious life even by some of those who defy the blacklisters to do their worst. The result will then be rationalized as real religion while in reality the spiritual life becomes fatally anemic through failure to engage the forces of this world.

It therefore becomes of the utmost importance to determine the nature and meaning of the present interest of the leaders of the Protestant churches in psychology, theology, and worship. Whether or not they constitute an abandonment of the incipient effort to make religion the saving force in civilization, whether or not they constitute the unconscious answer of organized religion to the demand that it become a servant of the powers that be, depends upon whether they are a substitute for the ethical emphasis in religion or an essential part of it.

The interest in psychology is different from that in theology and worship because it does not claim to be a primary interest of religion, but only asks us to use the aid of science in its educational and pastoral functions. This should be a great gain because it naturally leads to a better understanding of those unethical elements in modern society which produce torn and twisted personalities and nullify the educational efforts of religion by subjecting its pupils to the pressure of antireligious forces. But if it follows unwarily those dogmatic psychological cults which have chosen to ignore the social nature of personality and the pressure of economic environment upon the individual, then psychology in religion will repeat the story of a not inconsiderable section of psychology in the universities and become the effective instrument of those forces which are creating a social environment that inhibits and destroys personality. Without a consciousness of its part in the development of an ethical religion it will make individuals more efficient in maintaining the acquisitive society instead of more effective in transforming it.

Likewise, without a consciousness of the ethical demands of our religion the present interest in psychology will, like the former interest in philanthropy, absorb a section of the forces of religion in Red Cross work to the exclusion of an effort to stop the war. The necessity for specialization does not involve such futility as trying to cure the tubercular without a campaign for the prevention of tuberculosis as a social disease. Division of labor there must be, but also a common goal and strategy. Otherwise the current interest in psychology will help to keep a section of the forces of religion from hearing and accepting the challenge of an unethical society.

4. WHAT KIND OF GOD?

The relation of the present emphasis upon theology to the attempt to develop an ethical religion and to the demands of those who are attacking that movement is quite clear in so far as some preachers are concerned. They proclaim it a return to spiritual religion after a dangerous absorption in the practical aspects of life. Liberals who thus talk are at one point on common ground with their Fundamentalist foes; both of them possess an untrue and fatal psychological dualism, view an indivisible life as though it were in sections. Both of them also tend toward an interest in theology for its own sake, apart from its bearing upon the moral struggle. A revival of the old attempts to settle the problem of God apart from the problem of man is clearly a diversion of the forces of religion from the concrete challenge of current events, an attempt to give primacy again in theology to abstract reason.

Because of the basic antithesis between man's creative and critical faculties, he needs always in his mental development to beware of intellectualism with its consequent moral futility. When religion succumbs to this insidious disease an age is doomed. Surely there is enough historical record of what happens when speculative questions are the first interest of theology. When the intellects of the early church were more concerned with the composition of the deity than with his moral effectiveness there followed in due course, in the Papacy itself, lust and murder. When the Puritans ceased trying to make a religious community and became immersed in speculative theology, thereafter they helped to develop inhuman industry, antisocial finance, benevolent imperialism. A theology that is purely or predominantly metaphysical is foredoomed to lose in the struggle with sin, because it diverts man's energies elsewhere.

What then does it mean, especially after the social history of Unitarianism, that its left wing Humanists are more concerned with the abolition of God than with the attempt to secure opportunity for human development, that liberal theists are willing to argue with them concerning an issue which can only be demonstrated in ethical results. If the new interest in the problem of God is to expend itself in finding an argumentative answer to a godless Humanism, it is worse than a waste of time. It leaves the field of human living in possession of the enemies of religion while it seeks in words an answer to a perennial question whose only solution lies in ethical experience. By his fruits too is God also to be known.

There are, however, too many aspects to the present interest in the problem of God to put it down as mere intellectualism or to regard it as altogether the consequence of the moral defeatism into which the war threw the liberal wing of Protestantism. The Fundamentalist attack on the liberal position, or lack of one, would have compelled some answer without the belligerency developed by the war. Also there are other signs beside the revived interest in speculative theology that American culture is aging, and according to the manner of the past, is now ready to talk about what is behind the world it has hitherto been so busy subduing and exploiting. In the end, however, a people whose chief contribution to philosophy has been Pragmatism is not likely to remain unduly absorbed in theology for its own sake.

Underneath the present interest in the problem of God and its diverse expressions—humanist, metaphysical, and mystical—there run two compelling impulses. These various approaches to the problem are attempts to meet a moral need that has become imperious and to answer an intellectual challenge that cannot be ignored. Modern man is driven to seek God as much by his growing sense of failure in the organization of life as by the insistent pressure of science upon traditional beliefs.

The moral need is the less vocal, but it grows. In the decade before the great conflict, man with his science saw himself astride the world. He was predominantly conscious of himself as creator. Only occasionally did he glimpse himself as exploiter of nature and his fellow. Not at all did he see himself as the suicidal destroyer which the war showed him to be. In his prewar mood of pride, blithely sure that he was on the way to the Great Society, he did not need God—except to add to his self-satisfaction. Now seeing himself unable to achieve his ennobling desires, stricken with a sense of moral futility, he asks once again whether there is any help beyond himself. The outcome depends upon what kind of God is sought and for what purpose.

Most of our recent theological discussion is concerned with the cosmic question. It is seeking the God of nature. Its primary purpose is to solve an old intellectual problem, recently made more acute by science. It is conditioned more by the physical than by the social sciences. It is occupied more with the challenge of astronomy, physics, and chemistry than with that of biology, economics, and sociology. Thus when Wieman seeks God by the empirical method, the field of search is the relation of the behavior of man to the behavior of the universe. His behavior with his fellow in the social order is scarcely explored at all. The ethical problem is viewed mostly in personal terms, though manifestly the social order bears upon the individual somewhat as the cosmos does. Similarly when Barnes champions a humanistic religion for the sake of a scientific morality, although himself a social scientist, he is nevertheless more concerned with the God of nature than with the God of man. He is so engrossed in mutilating the corpse of scriptural cosmogony that he neglects to deal adequately with the fact that there are two aspects to the God of the Bible—He is variously an ethical being and a cosmic power. The question then, as now, is the relation between these two. Absorption in the cosmic problem is a symptom of an era of moral defeatism.

Inevitably an interest in theology that is centered in the cosmic aspect of the problem of God, that is preoccupied with nature as though it were something apart from human nature, comes out at one of two places. Sometimes it arrives with Whitehead at a metaphysical æstheticism, which sees the way to a moral universe but is inhibited by its approach from pursuing it, whose path leads to adoration but not to moral creativity. For those, who by temperament or training distrust the æsthetic impulse, the end of the search for the God of the cosmos apart from the God of man is absorption in the processes of the mind to the neglect of the practical needs of the unintellectual masses. This is the deepest treason of the intellectuals to humanity. The only way in which theology can escape becoming an accomplice of science in leading the masses into the bondage of a mechanized, money-making, order of life—in keeping them content with efficiency in the making, selling, and enjoying of creature comforts—is to continue the search for an ethical God whose presence can be practiced in the organized ways of human living, with whom men can coöperate in the working out of a real salvation from sins that are vividly concrete and terribly destructive.

Therefore, whether or not the current interest in the problem of God is an escape from the moral struggle depends upon whether it is primarily speculative or dynamic. Is it looking for God through the reason alone or through the total experience of man? Does it want to know Him merely for the satisfaction of its curiosity or in order to do His will? Does it want a God who can be luxuriously worshiped, and in other moods safely joked about; or a God powerful enough to make man change his ways—a revolutionary as well as an evolutionary God? Does it want to worship a God who is awe inspiring because He is the creative energy of a dynamic universe, who is terrible because of the consequences of failing to struggle with Him for the moralization of life, yet companionable because He is the power in us and between us that makes for righteousness and fellowship?

This does not mean that the choice before us is between an ethical or a cosmic religion in the sense that one or the other aspect of the problem of existence is left out. But it is a choice of priority of interest, between a religion whose first and chief concern is the challenging mystery of the universe of which we are a part, and a religion whose chief concern is the redemption and development of human nature in both its individual and corporate aspects.

It is only as we recognize and make this choice of

priority of interest that we have any chance of coming to terms with the cosmic problem, which for all our science is still mystery at the core. But the God of justice and righteousness, of mercy and fellowship at least is not the Unknowable. When theology addresses itself to the central and neglected issue of the relation between the Cosmic Energy and the Great Companion then it will find itself on the way toward achieving a synthesis of the ethical, the mystical, and the metaphysical experience of God. Ames in his last book, using the method of sociology for his approach, goes farther in this direction than any recent writer.

The question of order of interest is determining because if the cosmic problem, insoluble by reason alone, is put first the ethical problem is in the end neglected. These two have always been, and always will be, intertwined in the life of man and the story of religion. In the days of animism the main concern of religion was the daily practical interests of the tribe. When the gods appear, cosmic functions are mixed with their oversight of human affairs. When the one true God appears among the Hebrews, he is an ethical deity. There is good ground for holding that it is much later when a god of the cosmos is envisioned. Also it may be shown that as he engages interest the moral struggle is abandoned. If then, we are similarly diverted to-day we are repeating history instead of using it.

On the other hand, a primary interest in the relation of God to the moral struggle leads directly into an interest in the cosmic problem. Any increase of certainty or of faith in that direction can only come, as it has in the past, through a gain in ethical experience. The God of the prophets and of Jesus, the god of the seers and the saints, is to be further known only through ethical action. Whatever certainty is attainable in the religious life is now to be achieved by aid of the social rather than the physical sciences. It is the weakness of current theology that it is looking to dubious compromises with the natural sciences for support which is both weak and temporary, whereas its real strength can come only through a moral use of what is demonstrable concerning the improvability of man.

It is time for theology to put the cosmic problem on the table for awhile as unfinished business, to be taken up again when the state of civilization is less urgent. If it does not, it will be ignored by a world whose more pressing matters will not wait. What cannot be known about the nature of the cosmos can be borne, but an inhuman world is unendurable. The essential question about the cosmic energy is whether it is on the side of or indifferent to the achievement of a moral order. That can never be discovered by the processes of logic, useful as they are for verification. What man needs most to know can be found out only by acting on the assumption that it may be so, by assuming an ethical God as a working hypothesis. If that effort falls short of certainty, it will nevertheless bring man something better than the moral nihilism or the æsthetic futility that wait upon a purely intellectual interest in the cosmic problem.

5. THE PRICE OF BEAUTY

At the present moment, however, the Protestant denominations are more concerned with beautifying the buildings and services of religion than they are with the problem of God. Costly Gothic churches are rising all over the land and the prominent theme of discussion among the nonliturgical denominations is the improvement of worship. Akin to this rise of religious æstheticism is the renaissance of mysticism. Divergent as is their expression of it, a reliance upon the leading of the emotions ties together in one family the Quaker, the Anglo-Catholic, and the Holy Roller. All of them, with their various cousins, have had their innings since the war, as was to be expected after that emotional upheaval. With neither Quaker nor Anglo-Catholic, however, has the emotional satisfaction in religion been divorced from the practical problems of life. The latter have their Socialist wing and the former have added to their historic stand against war, mighty works of relief and reconstruction in the war stricken lands. Also, particularly in England, some of them have come to close grips with the thorny question of the management and ownership of industry.

Admittedly the mystic element is a permanent and necessary factor in religion. Never was it more needed than in this machine, jazz age, and never did it have less chance of development than in these days of the salesman, the committee, and the convention, when privacy is so invaded and destroyed that one has small chance to be alone with himself or with God. It is equally apparent that the mystic emphasis in religion apart from the ethical attack upon all the problems of current life not only fails to conquer the machine age, it does not even escape from it. The quietist wins no victory in the modern world. India needs and will have the machine, so Gandhi has yet to find out what to do with it. The Quakers having found that godliness with contentment is great gain have now to learn, with the rest of us, what to do with property. The mystic approach to God leads us away from reality unless it takes us into the moral struggle. The insight of emotional experience must justify and verify itself in action, then it leads to further insight.

The demand among us for beauty in religion is part of the wider demand for more beauty and joy in life. It is a sign that the crudity of the frontier has passed. The city stage has been reached. Man is concerned less with nature and more with art. The cult of beauty is a part of the pursuit of culture, which is in large measure the attempt to buy it. Also it is a joint revolt against the Puritan and the machine, an effort to break the mechanistic rigidity in which they have jointly encased life.

One aspect of the present exaltation of beauty in religious circles is the fact that some of our younger intellectuals with a Methodist, Baptist, or Presbyterian background have suddenly discovered the Greeks—or at least one side of them, for they seem to have overlooked the Attic religion of civic obligation and the Spartan discipline. By a similarly partial psychology these insurgent youths have been taught to extol self-realization. They have suddenly learned what religion should have taught them before, that life is to be enjoyed as well as changed. So time has its revenge on the Puritans. Duty with beauty left out is replaced by beauty with duty ignored. As for sacrifice, that remains mostly for those who cannot know either the Greeks or Freud, and for them it is compulsory and vicarious. Once again the motto is, "Let joy be unrestrained," and the core of the problem—which is the nature of joy and its consequences—is left untouched, even by that new and vague absolute, Science. So the old question emerges for the new gospel to answer—how does the devotee of self-realization avoid the easy descent into Avernus.

Some of the elders too have been making a discovery, or perhaps remembering something they learned from the Greeks long ago but had forgotten in a beauty fearing religious environment—that there is a relationship between the good, the true, and the beautiful. Since the popular cry among the emancipated is that beauty is the great moral sanction and test, that discipline and penalties are out of date along with sin, there is an effort in the pulpit to make the good life attractive by telling about the charm of it. But this is something which had better be demonstrated rather than talked about. For the talk runs at times dangerously near the fallacy, "Be pretty and you will be virtuous," which is the twin of that other half truth so dear to sentimental preachers, "Be good and you will be happy."

There is also a practical need behind the current cult of religious beauty. It was certainly time in this country to improve church architecture and to remove the crudities and banalities of many of our assemblies for worship, to refine the rough and ready manners of a pioneer people. Also, it was necessary to repent and forsake the sins of the Puritan against beauty in the name of morals, which were almost as deep as the sins of the Cavalier against morals in the name of joy. The more drabness the standardization of the machine forces upon us, the more necessary it is that beauty should be cultivated. Even profit seeking business is discovering this. What could a purposeful economic organization not do, backed by a free, vital art and a dynamic religion, to express even in the products of the machine that insatiable desire of man for form and color which now finds such paltry expression as the strutting of the fraternal orders in pinchbeck mummery of dead days.

So the cult of the Gothic must face the test of its relation to the life of to-day. Does this use of a religious art form of the past signify the failure of both art and religion to grapple with current problems, does it reveal their joint lack of creativity? Does it mean that the industrial age has not yet achieved enough ethical reality in its social living to produce its own religious architecture? The question is not answered by pointing to the genuine beauty of some Gothically crowned skyscrapers. They are an impossible hybrid, born of an unnatural union of borrowed art with original finance, seldom noticed by the scurrying throngs below and then only with discomfort, because both land and time must be used first of all to make money.

The Gothic in the industrial age, put on a steel frame, is divorced from both its economic and spiritual environment. In its beginning it was the expression of a community, the outward and visible sign of its spiritual aspiration, expressing the degree of its ordered and coöperative living. In England of the sixteenth and nineteenth, as in America of the twentieth century, its revised forms signified mostly that much money had recently been made and its pious owners, stimulated by energetic ecclesiasts, were able to get churches built—to order. If our current reproduction of the Gothic is something more than a display of money and energy, if it does express a genuine desire to know God and to share him with others, it remains to be demonstrated that its quest can be any more successful than the search of the beauty parlor for that which only healthful living can supply.

The plain fact remains that our Gothic revival expresses only the aspiration of those who have the money to pay for it, and that is a limited circle even within the household of faith. These new, expensive, and sometimes beautiful churches are placed mostly in the suburbs. They are physically and socially inaccessible to most of the wage earners. They are predominantly for the people who live by salaries and profits. Thus curiously enough, capitalistic industrialism in a supposedly democratic era has managed to reverse the situation of the feudal days which produced the Gothic it now imitates. Then authority was rigidly stratified. But, while there was separation in social and political status, there was community in worship. Now there is community in political status but growing separation in worship. This latter fact is both a consequence and a further cause of the social cleavages and political inequalities that economic forces and conditions are creating.

The community has no sense of ownership in these modern cathedrals, and the few attempts to make them civic enterprises are foredoomed because they start from a fictitious base. These buildings belong to private and limited corporations. With the best will in the world on the part of their owners to use them for the service of all men or to have all men use them for the worship of God, it simply cannot be done. The physical and social barriers are impassable, save for an insignificant few. For most of the poor, who dwell elsewhere, there is another kind of building, service, and preacher. To the organized workers our new churches like new battleships mean jobs.

At least this consideration, in a world in which unemployment grows, obscures the expression of religion in the one case and of irreligion in the other. Here is tragedy enough in the making. Is it then to go on to its climax unperceived by those seekers for the good life whose eyes are held by a vision of beauty which too late they will find to be fatally deceptive?

Our modern replicas of the Gothic are adding hundreds of millions to the vested interest of organized religion in a property system which is increasingly demonstrating itself to be antisocial. How much then will their very beauty but increase the tolerance of worshipers with the injustices of the present order? These new buildings are one product of our recent financial expansion, paid for out of its profit and dividends. But this new income is concentrated among a fraction of the population. Yet into it has gone some fragment of the lives of many toilers in many parts of the world. Some of this indirectly confiscated human energy has then been transferred to these new churches. There is, therefore, in them an element of forced labor analogous to that which powerful ecclesiasts and barons compelled into some of the cathedrals of the past. Whose right was it thus to take away and to give? And whose name will ever be blessed when the loss is perceived? According to the laws of history, which this generation may too late discover to have that dread certainty which their forefathers ascribed to the laws of God, these structures are insecure to the extent to which injustice has entered their foundations. Therefore, it is historically certain that, unless they are used to transform the economic conditions which made them possible, to those who will finally accomplish that transformation neither their beauty nor their religion will make any more appeal than did that of the Russian churches to the Bolsheviks or that of England's cathedrals to Cromwell's troopers.

A similar question arises concerning the present interest in the development of beauty in church services. Is it under our conditions, like beauty in church buildings, the possession only of the cultured and well-to-do? It has not been so owned in the Greek, Roman, Anglican, and Lutheran churches which root back into the days when religion was a community force. But under the *régime* of capitalistic industrialism, beauty in worship tends to accompany wealth and the type of culture that depends upon it. There is a well known tendency for families which acquire money to leave the churches of simple ways for those whose more elaborate forms involve also more social distinction. In the nonliturgical denominations it is among the preachers of the wealthier and suburban churches that the trend toward ritualism is most marked. In the same circles appears also an inclination toward mysticism, without the vow of poverty. Is this an attempt to possess God as well as the goods and powers of the world? Does its development involve a transformation of the God of faith, like that which the acquisitive society has accomplished with nature, into the hireling of a class —a Master Robot?

The relationship of the present interest in beautifying religious services to the current demand for the subordination of religion to the powers that control this world turns of course upon the purpose and content of worship. Again the issue has already been settled for those preachers who hail this emphasis as a return to real religion after an attempt to substitute the service of man for the worship of God. As if Jesus, like the prophets before him, had not made it sufficiently clear that the service of man is an aspect of the worship of God, the aspect moreover which determines its reality! If the purpose of worship is but to pay an absolute sovereign his due tribute, if its content is only adoration and praise duly interspersed with petitions for special privilege, then according to the founders of our religion to make it more beautiful is only to make it more useless, to increase the impossibility of its ever finding a God who has no reality apart from ethical experience.

The greater the ethical need of the community, the more immoral and irreligious is such worship. By the seductive power of beauty it not only keeps men from the moral battlefield when the fight is in the balance, it also betrays man's highest aspirations and possibilities for fellowship into the treason of becoming a separating force. When the effect of beautiful religious buildings and services is to keep people content with an unjust and unholy social order, to provide them with means of escape from unethical situations which can and ought to be changed, it signifies that religion has become refined, sophisticated, decadent—a corrupting force in a dying age. It means that for the appearance of genuine beauty in religion, as in art, all forms of culture must move into another phase by a change in the economic base of society upon which they depend.

If then beauty is to strengthen and not diminish the power of religion to aid the moral growth of mankind it must be so used in worship as to increase the desire to get rid of economic injustice and social unrighteousness, to stimulate the longing for holiness in the individual and the community. The degree to which it can do this is the degree to which it can make vivid and compelling those concrete needs and obligations which in an ethical religion become increasingly the content of worship, to whose satisfaction in moments of crisis worship itself must give way, recognizing that then a further experience of God waits upon action.

It is the joint function of religion and art to give men release from the burden of the actual by transporting them through imaginative insight into the ideal. Art calls with the beauty of form, color and tone, religion with the beauty of holiness. Neither is true to itself when it provides enervating escape from the struggle of life instead of temporary and energizing release. But religion has a further responsibility than art. Its function is never to provide recreation—as art may legitimately do—but always re-creation. Art reaches its highest form when it too takes on the function of religion and relates dynamically the two worlds in which man lives—the ideal and the actual. Hence the test of worship, and its only justification, is its capacity for bringing the power of the unseen world into which it transports its worshipers to bear upon their world of daily contacts, its ability to put the life of the ages into the moral struggle of the moment and so transmute the highest potencies of the present into continuing values.

To put the matter in its sharpest form, the present cult of the Gothic and of ritual offers us the choice between an ethical and an æsthetic religion just as the interest in the problem of God faces us with the choice between an ethical and a cosmic religion. Again however, it is not an either-or dilemma. Once more it is a question of order and proportion between elements which are always present in some degree in all religions, because they correspond to indelible needs of human nature. The issue is which aspect of religion is to be primary and regulative, to give the others their tone and color. Is religion to be first of all ethical, intellectual, or devotional? It is possible to develop either of the two latter elements without the former. Indeed it has often been done with disastrous results. But an ethical religion cannot be developed without due place accorded to theology and to worship. Because man is a thinking animal he cannot be moral unless he wrestles with the problem of his relation to the universe as well as to his fellow, because he is an insatiable lover of beauty he cannot achieve ethical living without due place for æsthetic satisfactions. But in an ethical religion, theology and worship have moral content and aim.

6. THE ISSUES MERGE

The fact that an ethical religion involves a continuous attempt to transform the world and itself, while an intellectual or æsthetic religion is increasingly at home in the world and content with itself, makes it plain that the choice of American Protestantism concerning the kind of religion it is going to develop will determine its answer to the choice now being thrust upon it concerning its relation to the political-economic order. The position it will finally occupy relative to the principalities and powers of this world, as also the extent of its capacity to strengthen and console persons in the disasters of life, will be settled by the decision as to which of its own elements shall have primacy—the desire to understand the nature of the universe, the longing to enjoy life, or the imperative to change it.

This choice is of vital significance for the social order because it carries with it a judgment concerning which aspects of experience should have primacy in society—the immediate or the continuing, the separating or the uniting, the sectional or the universal. Thus it is the opportunity of religion, in and through its own course as a social institution and not through any temporal power, to help American society—now halfway between democracy and empire—decide whether it wants to be acquisitive or spiritual, possessive or creative, class-divided or fraternal. Failing this, American Protestantism becomes on the one hand what the blacklisters want it to be—the sanction and ally of the new economic imperialism, and on the other hand what some of its own leaders desire for it—an escape from a sordid and unjust world into music and incense, vague rhetoric and emotional exaltation.

The consequences that hang upon this choice have been written enough times into the human record so that there is now no excuse for taking a course without knowing where it will come out. Time and again, in many lands, whenever religion has become absorbed in abstract questions or gorgeous ceremonies, its devotees have thereafter become corrupt with greed and lust in a corrupted world. In our own religious history there are sufficient instances to show how religion becomes a part of the power of this world when it ceases trying to change it. The last of these was when Protestantism yielded the moral sovereignty of the world of economic affairs to natural law and allowed selfishness to be established as a secular religion.

[53]

The usual explanation for this abdication is that the teachings of religious morality were inadequate because they were expressed as static rules instead of dynamic principles. But the fact also remains that the churches were busy about other things. Theology and ritual and organization were their consuming concerns.

What then is to be the present and final attitude of our religion toward the new imperial power which it has permitted to assert absolute sovereignty? Is it content to become another court chaplain, whose ministrations produce a humane spirit within certain areas but do not change the nature of the organization, do not alter its basic dependence upon greed and force? Or will it proclaim a new order of life? Standing before this choice the leaders of our churches may well remember that the last writer in the Bible calls mighty Rome the "Great Harlot" because he sees her seducing, wasting, and destroying the life of man. From age to age imperial powers change their form but not their nature. If religion then develops into sanction instead of judgment for the modern empire of money it thereby becomes Chief Pander to the lusts of man instead of the means to his salvation.

CHAPTER II

The Need for an Ethical Religion

1. THE STATE OF PUBLIC MORALS

IF the future course of American Protestantism could now be deliberately charted and then followed without deflecting pressure from historic habits and vested interests, its direction would be determined by surveying the needs of modern life. This method, already largely used in shaping the programs of churches in local communities, and in lesser degree the activities of their national and international associations, is an acceptance by organized religion of the functional test which the machine age applies to all human institutions. Also it realizes the peculiar genius of the Christian religion, whose original distinguishing characteristic was that it proclaimed salvation for man. To have meaning in the modern world this must be salvation from current evil. In working out such a salvation lies the answer to the much discussed question of the terms on which the modern man can be religious.

On this basis then the choice of the churches concerning which aspect of religion is to be central, and thus their answer to the powers of this world that now demand their submission, would be determined by the predominant human need. Since the issue at stake is the corporate function of religion, the question that needs first to be asked is what is the condition of our corporate life. While theology is debating whether the ethical or the cosmic problem is its first concern, while the churches are deciding whether improving their forms of worship or the life of man is their main business, what is the state of our moral health? Are we moving so steadily toward righteousness, justice, and fellowship—that is, toward the experience of an ethical God in the working out of an ethical salvation—that we can now put first on our agenda the cosmic problem? Is the beauty of holiness so established in our midst that we can relax into a beauty of worship that raises no disturbing moral issues?

Any attempt to answer these questions must recognize that the basic fact in the life of the United States since the war is the increase of money-making. With the exception of one short break we have in the language of the politicians enjoyed a period of unexampled prosperity. It is well known that this is the most potent of the factors determining our political situation. The relation of our recent large and easy money-making to the rest of our life particularly to the tone and trend of our moral attitudes and judgments has not been so generally analyzed.

The most influential aspects of our new wealth and income are its concentration and its source. It is conceded now by publications which speak for the owning and employing sections of the population that our recent monetary gains have been unevenly distributed both within the business world and outside it. While with much labor the statisticians demonstrate a considerable gain in real income for a section of the wage earners, while living standards have gone up over a wider area through the spread of installment buying, there are yet several millions on the farms and in industry who have not shared in this increased purchasing power. Meanwhile the rich have been getting richer. Our metropolitan papers are beginning to count as millionaires only those with an annual income of a million, of whom there are now as many hundreds as there were scores before the war. While millions of people of small income are better off than they were before, and better off than other millions in their own class, yet in relation to that section of the population whose income is above ten thousand dollars they are worse off. This is the camel we have swallowed while straining over the gnat of a limited increase in real income. Inequality between income groups has been increased and this is what finally counts most in fixing the attitudes between the classes by which the stability of a social order is determined.

Already this increased equality between income groups shows its natural results in an expansion of the leisure class and of class consciousness, both of them traditionally regarded by us as morally undesirable and recognized as the preludes to class antagonism, which we have always believed ourselves able to avoid. To-day it is the class consciousness of the well-to-do that grows in our midst; to-morrow it will be the class consciousness of the workers which now has to be artificially stimulated. The fact that the appeal to exclusiveness has recently acquired a definite advertising value is only one of many signs which indicate that the early equalitarian tendency of this nation is definitely checked. The American philosophy of equality is now an academic subject, a clear indication that its value is more historical than current. It is well that this generation should challenge the pious sentimentalism which is content with affirming that all men are created free and equal, but what is gained, even in intellectual integrity, by a mere negation which blinks the essential fact that equal right to life, liberty, and the pursuit of happiness is being effectually denied by economic limitations, upheld in court decisions, and enforced with all the powers of the state? Both affirmation and negation are means of escaping the ugly fact that disparity of culture, now as in the past, follows disparity of income, that opportunities for development become stratified by the inheritance of environment as do capacities by the transmission of tendencies toward disability. It is inevitable, as a comparison of Eastern and Western universities reveals, that with growing inequality of income the right to a college education becomes more and more a class possession to be jealously guarded and the desire and capacity for it becomes disproportionately distributed.

Thus it is no accident that the spread in our universities of those academic versions of the Ku Klux Klan—the Nordic myth and its twin the intelligence cult—coincides with our recent increased inequality of income. The superiority complex of the alleged intellectuals is a defense reaction. It is a vain barrier to protect their children against competition from the barbarian hordes below. It is the proclamation of the latest monopoly—a corner in brains and character—as futile as it is false. Some day perhaps the intellectuals will achieve sufficient intelligence to see that the only adequate defense of the good life for anybody is to make it possible for everybody. Then they will have an intelligent and ethical base for the necessary program of population limitation.

Meanwhile our new found wealth has the same divisive tendencies in the world at large that it produces within our own boundaries. When the money made out of the war changed us from a debtor to a creditor nation, when the billions we have been able to invest overseas made us dictator of the destiny of a large part of the world, the attitudes between us and the other nations involved began to change. As we grow richer—in part at their expense—resentment and jealousy on their side, fear and suspicion on ours, arise to check the sentimental desire for international concord which is our traditional attitude toward the old world. Trotsky is right when he points out in his autobiography that the most significant fact for the immediate future of human history is the changed relationship of the United States and Europe.

The new nationalism that we have acquired since the war is plainly colored by our recent orgy of money-making. Our new financial prestige and power have given it a vigor which the stimulus of the conflict alone could not have produced. Our old nationalism was rooted in a dying tradition. Its manifestation was a spread-eagle, complacent assurance that our institutions were better than those of Europe, at which the Old World could afford to smile. The new variety is shaped by present economic conditions. The man in the street is thrilled on occasion by being told that he belongs to the wealthiest and most efficient nation in the world. He shares vicariously in its prestige and power and is ready to defend them. Thus the new nationalism becomes intensely chauvinistic, and therefore dangerous. The highest tariff and the biggest navy in the world are its extreme demands. Its achievements are the Smoot-Hawley bill and parity, both of them disastrous to the goodwill and threatening to the peace of the world.

The vigorous militarism that is the twin of our new nationalism derives its strength from the same source. The demand for preparedness reduces finally in any conversation, especially among the unsophisticated, to the simple idea that we are now a very wealthy people living in a very wicked world which will take our possessions away from us unless we can defend them. The necessity of protecting our wealth begins to take the place in our political discussions that defense of trade routes has long occupied in those of Britain. In a more circuitous way the vociferous demand of our patriotic societies for larger armaments is tied in with the defense of social prestige and the property upon which that now mostly rests. Hence their animus against the Reds. When the threat of the Russian Revolution is put on top of our new financial eminence, we have again an incitement to militarism which the experience of the war alone could not supply. This is demonstrated beyond dispute in the manual of instruction for citizenship in use in summer training camps which inculcates definite views and attitudes on the economic question.

According to the historic law that the vanquished impose some of their habits upon the conquerors we acquired a militaristic tendency in the conflict. Naturally enough a certain proportion of the civilians who were inducted into military procedure became enamored of uniforms, title, and authority, especially those who could not hope to have prestige in civil life. This tendency has been kept alive and increased by the National Defense Act—a product of war time fears—which gives us through military training in high schools and colleges, citizens training camps and Reserve Officers Corps, allied with official fostering of Reserve Officers Associations and persistently successful efforts to militarize the Boy Scouts, the most powerful and subtle system ever possessed by any nation for disseminating through the civilian population the twin doctrines of the inevitability of war and the necessity of preparedness. Our real military leaders know that as actual preparation for war this training is negligible, for the next war will be decided by aircraft and chemicals. But as moral preparedness they count it great gain. What they are seeking to do is to change the moral values and attitudes of a pacific people.

Against this developing militarism there operates our traditional desire for goodwill now reinforced by the new idea of peace born of a realization of the consequences of war and the inadequacy and danger of traditional conceptions of patriotism and security. Thus the propaganda of the seekers after peace counters the offensive of the believers in the inevitability of war, and the nation confusedly wavers between pacts renouncing war as an instrument of policy, attempts to reduce navies, conscription bills, military training and refusal of citizenship to those who will not promise to fight. Underneath, moving desperately to pull down the scale, is the unseen force of our new billions of paper wealth, with its legal claims to income concentrated in a fraction of the people but scattered around the earth. Its influence was recently voiced by an editorial writer whose words are daily read by millions. Commenting upon an article which had pointed out that the decisive battle of the next war would be fought in the air and decided in about two hours, he says,

"Can anything be done? Certainly. The richest country in the world might have such power of attack as would mean swift destruction for any nation foolish enough to attack the United States."

Our new militaristic nationalism is after all only an aspect of a larger fact—our economic imperialism, whose purpose is the collection of revenue through investment. The transformation of our experiment in democracy into an empire of finance was predetermined by our possession of so much of the world's store of natural resources and our development of them under the capitalist economy, whose virtues have been stimulated and its vices unperceived by our religion. The financial opportunity of the World War was the climactic event in a course of empire that began when we took Hawaii.

The American Empire is now a factual commonplace in the writings of our historians and political scientists. It is not yet a part of the consciousness of the common people as the empire is in Britain. From them it is still concealed by the Pickwickian phrases of those we elect to speak for us, just as the increase of effortless and antisocial property rights is camouflaged by pious talk about efficiency and service. It is hard to believe that these elected persons can be as ignorant as they seem when they affirm that we are not imperialistic because we desire no further territory and our dependencies give us not profit but duty. But such cant cannot long cover up the hard fact that the American empire of investment is gradually succeeding the British empire of trade. It has the selfsame assurance of righteousness and benevolence. It does not practice intervention, it lends the marines. It does not interfere with the destiny of any other nation, it only puts their finances under American controllers with the final word in New York. Where the Pax Britannica—like its predecessor in Rome—justified itself to itself by establishing law and order, the Pax Americana approves itself—again to itself—by publishing abroad the glad tidings of the gospel of prosperity, graciously telling its dependencies that this is more to be desired than the self-government we refuse them. Thus the liberty that now enlightens a part of the world from these shores is freedom to keep a minor share of the profit we so kindly assist them to make for us. It is obvious that if these situations become the accepted manner of life for this country a considerable change in moral climate will have occurred.

Parallel with our recent development of militarism and imperialism is the increasing repression of civil liberties. In the decade since the war there have been more limitations put around freedom of speech, press, and assemblage by laws, ordinances, court decisions, administrative orders, mob action, and the cultivation of intolerance and the boycott than at any previous period of our history. This was to be expected after the operation of the Espionage Act in war time followed by the alarm awakened by the Russian upheaval. England went through a similar experience after the French Revolution. But there is another cause at work prolonging the hangover from the war and darkening the shadow cast upon this hemisphere by events in Russia. It is significant that the largest number of interferences with civil liberty occur in the areas of industrial conflict, that repression is exerted mostly against those who seek to change the current conception and practice of property rights. It is again our newly won, concentrated wealth that needs protection and is afraid to trust itself to the democratic process.

There is a common point at which the imperialists, the militarists, and the money-makers meet in the repression of civil liberties and provide a common force operating against those who oppose war, criticize foreign policy, discuss economic change or resist industrial autocracy. The organizations which make the blacklists, interfere with meetings, incite the authorities to hunt down the Reds, and carry on the campaign against radicalism also agitate for bigger and better armaments. They are an alliance composed of patriotic and military associations and industrial propaganda agencies. It is a natural union of militaristic patriotism and property privilege. As the industrialists gradually took on propaganda against the pacifists the militarists developed a campaign against the Bolshevists. If property rights are to be protected regardless of their social utility, repression and then abrogation of constitutional liberties of discussion are as essential as armaments.

Other developments of similar moral import follow inevitably upon the nature of our recent money-making. Unlike the increase of money and credit that followed the Civil War most of it has come not from the development of natural resources, new commodities, or markets, but from new combinations of existing business made primarily for investment gains. Most of the returns of this new found wealth have to be listed in the "Unearned Income" column of the income tax return. Most of its capital carries increased charges for dividends with no corresponding addition to plant. This is especially true in the power industry which is so vital to the possibility of a new order of living. For most of the population, in their capacity

[64]

both as producer and consumer, this new capital represents debt not wealth. In so far as this debt is to be paid by one section of our population to another, it means that some millions of children in both industrial and agricultural regions will, like their parents, continue to live below a comfort and health standard. In so far as this debt is due to our investors from other countries, it means that a portion of the energy of those who already live on a lower scale than we do is devoted to increasing the comforts and luxuries of that section of our population which already lives above a health and comfort standard.

Acceptance of unearned income, living at the expense of others, is contrary to the economic morality of a productive people. When this practice is accepted it means that the economic base of morals has shifted from production to exploitation, from return for service rendered to that which luck enables the fortunate, or skill the stronger, to take. Thus both among those who take it and those who pay it much of the tribute now disguised under circuitous forms of profit and interest is deprived of any moral worth and loses claim to moral respect. The ethical base of property has been undermined by the growth of unearned income. When the change is sufficiently accomplished and the nature of the fact sufficiently understood, of what use will be the self-deception that now justifies the jailing of Communists under laws that forbid talking and writing, no matter how impractically, about the overthrow of government by force and violence? The nature of functionless wealth is still more threatening to the stability of society than is its concentration. It is immoral in the final analysis because it is socially impossible.

The extent to which the ethic of speculative gain is displacing in our economic life the ethic of socially useful labor can be easily seen in any community by testing the attitudes of people toward easy money as against that which comes from hard and useful effort. Along with the banker, professional men, merchants, wage earners, farmers—all show signs of the corrupting desire to get something for nothing. The movement for efficiency, the tendency toward improvement of service, has an uphill fight against the increasing willingness to get by and the common approval of what one can get away with. A college daily comments on the prevalence of cheating in examinations and the tolerant attitude of the community including some of the faculty, who are said to regard it with amusement. This Dives among the nations has not the same use for the spirit of labor that he had before he became swollen with riches.

A more concrete example of the influence of our moral standards of the recent increase of unearned income is the general attitude toward political corruption. During and after a war it is certain that the public treasury will be looted. It was in the Civil War period that the foundations of organized corruption in both our business and politics were laid. This time the loot was as much larger as were the opportunities. Not half of the story was or ever will be publicly told. Yet not the amount of the plundering but the attitude toward it—the silence of high-minded men in public life, the apathy of the common people, the cynicism of the intellectuals—is the measure of our public morality. Not in our time has it fallen as low.

Again this is more than the natural consequence of war exhaustion. The fact that no reform movement makes headway indicates a more serious malady. Business for profit has naturally produced politics for profit. The leaders of business were blackmailed by political gangsters. In self-defense they learned how to use them. Now they tend to enter politics directly and the two worlds become more and more one. It is the inevitable development of a system of life that honors preëminently success in money-making and teaches men that something for nothing is most to be desired. In such a world the little grafters imitate the big money-makers both in seeking easy money and in using the processes of government for that purpose. They justify themselves on the ground of getting their share and if their schemes get big enough, give them the cloak of patriotism. The confusion of motives and ends manifest by those who testified in the oil lease cases represents a very large section of the interlocked world of government and private money-making.

This merging of patriotism and profit is accelerated by the extent to which our government in its foreign as well as domestic policies is engaged in helping business to make money. It gives no such protection to the customer as it gives to the business man, no such standing before the law to labor. It will not relieve trade unions from intolerable abuses of the injunction process. It will not make public the findings of its Bureau of Standards, and so bring vast savings to the buying public, because that would also injure business. When it tries to protect the consumer by regulating public utilities it largely fails because its courts are afraid of injuring the property rights of the possessing class. The moral corruption that follows the fallacy that the way to aid the underlying population is to help the business men make profits is nowhere better seen than in the votes of some senators on the recent tariff bill. Men who could not be touched by dollars were bought by the political value of profit favors to some local industry.

If we make any gains in cleansing our political machinery they are more than discounted by the results of the closer connection between business and politics. We put millionaires in office and congratulate ourselves that they are beyond the need of graft, but their political philosophy—inherited from the eighteenth century—is that government exists to help business because business exists to serve the people—by making all the money it can legitimately. So they develop administrative, and influence legislative and judicial policies, to that end. Thus instead of a frontal attack upon political corruption we refine the process and increase the source. We exchange the coarser and lesser corruption for one more subtle and pervasive. These changes in our standards of public morality—the tacit acceptance of political corruption as inevitable, the increasing use and recognition of government as a servant of money-making business, the growth of the attitudes and practices of nationalism, militarism, and imperialism— mark a critical point in the story of this people. They are signs that American life is become mature and sophisticated. They are the early symptoms of the disease of civilizations, a disease which has always proved fatal. The other symptom whose appearance is the unfailing sign of approaching degeneracy is not absent—the growth of artificially cultivated licentiousness. The undue stimulation of sex appetite in a wealthy and wealth-seeking society is altogether different in its nature and consequences from the free or less conventional expression of primitive peoples. As antidote there is among us a struggle for a healthy development in sex morals, from ignorant blundering to intelligent control, from the bondage of woman to her independence. But there is also a tendency to view sex relations as solely the concern of the individuals participating in them. This is ethical anarchy, for the essence of morality is social responsibility. Which of these tendencies prevails, whether or not we succumb to antisocial sex habits, depends upon whether we recognize and eliminate the artificial stimulation of sex appetites by the money-making spirit and the conditions of life which it creates.

The failure to appreciate the import and recognize the cause of the recent changes in our moral standards is exemplified in two contiguous attitudes current among our intellectuals. It is a fashion to dismiss the critics of our industrial society as deluded voices crying for the outworn virtues of a simpler agricultural society, the useless standards of a deficient economic period. Likewise there is a cult proclaiming the saving power of the machine and the engineer. Mechanism has for some of our moderns the same capacity for achieving the salvation of man that their grandfathers attributed to Almighty God and their fathers to irresistible evolution. This deification of the machine is accomplished by a fatal combination of sophistication and faith. Of course, we cannot go back to simpler days nor to their standards. But the vital question is can we develop the virtues of socially useful labor that were the strength of a more rugged agricultural society, and the mutual exchange of goods, services, and opportunities that was the cohesion of the periods of economic deficit, in the present days of division of labor and surplus.

This is what no previous civilization has been able to do. And none has survived that failure. For the conquest of life lies in the development, not the repetition, of the moral experience of smaller, simpler groups in larger and more complex associations. To secure this is, in any age and land, one of the prophetic tasks of religion.

Those who assume that there is an essential saving virtue in the machine process and the scientific method that will synthesize the strength of the peasant and the graces of the cosmopolitan, that will redeem society from the stolidity of the one and the decadence of the other, are making a heavy overdraft on blind faith. So far in the American scene, where the machine is most dominant, the battle has been going against us. We are slowly reversing our moral standards and adopting those qualities of an older world which we have hitherto regarded as vices, which history and not the prejudice of boors declares to cause the destruction of civilization. Those who take the machine age on trust are therefore only helping us toward disaster. Their naïve faith overlooks the fact that the machine is directed by the acquisitive society, that its subordination to money-making has not only inhibited its capacity to enable the Great Society but, by the new agencies it has provided for imperialism and the new occasions for class conflict it has furnished, has terribly increased the destructive passions and habits of mankind. With all its respect for intelligence and its desire for goodwill, what saving health can industrial society show to offset its increase of unearned income, luxury habits, class antagonism, and the kind of property rights which no previous possessors have ever been able finally to collect or enforce?

2. HOW CAN MODERN MAN BE RELIGIOUS?

Thus the basic fact which should determine the program of organized religion is that American society is on the way, all unaware, to repeat the sins of past civilizations whose manifest wages are death. Unless these evils are recognized when they first appear as the symptoms of a disease which unchecked always proves fatal, their development cannot be prevented. If they are to be stopped, it can only be done, as in the case of tuberculosis, in the incipient stages.

Does this demand of current life upon the resources of religion appear any different if the situation is viewed from the standpoint of the traditional concern of Christianity with the individual, if we ask on what terms the modern man—that is the man bred and born in the intellectual climate produced by science—can be religious? First of all, and last of all this question means on what terms can he pursue holiness—that is wholeness—both within himself and in his relations to the universe. How can he overcome the evil that mutilates and destroys? In the order of business for religion this issue always takes precedence over the cosmic problem and imperatively so in times of moral crisis like these. True the riddle of the universe also has its imperative, but in moments of peril intellectual curiosity is out of place.

What the modern man needs to know about the universe is whether it is hostile, indifferent, or friendly to his moral aspirations and struggle. That he discovers by uniting faith and action not by intellectualizing. The intellectual need is negative rather than positive, that religion should not contradict what science demonstrates concerning the nature and behavior of the universe. The quicker religion is content to leave to science and philosophy those aspects of the nature of man and the universe concerning which it formerly spoke with authoritative ignorance, the sooner it will be able to coördinate its work with theirs, prevent them from being unmoral or becoming immoral, and so help modern man to such wholeness of life and outlook as is now possible. Also by making ethical development its first concern organized religion will be able the more rapidly to aid the modern spirit to recovery from that paralysis of the moral will whose chief cause is its refusal to attack the moral problem because it cannot now read all mystery.

When he seeks after righteousness the modern man finds that all the sins that beset him are tied in with the evils that threaten civilization, which corrupt him even as he strengthens them; he discovers that he can move toward holiness only as he becomes intelligently aware of their causes and strives to eliminate them. He finds his salvation not in running away from the city of destruction but in helping to prevent the evils that are destroying it. Failing this, he is indeed lost, because he has eaten of the fruit of the tree of knowledge. Knowing what he knows, facing possibilities that have come to no other generations, if he neglects to use his knowledge to make a new world, he is of all men the most miserable. He has fallen not from any original state of innocence but from the high estate of intelligence and capacity. He has missed the opportunity to live creatively, and descended into the company of the destroyers.

As for the masses whose destiny it has ever been to suffer and die unaware of what life may be, they can only live religiously if they are awakened to the possibilities of human existence and become willing to pay the price of their development. This is the vital germ of good in the great Russian upheaval, that human beings who have been little more than beasts of burden are now becoming conscious makers of a new society. Salvation for the crowd in this country means transforming its members from mere consumers of standardized comforts, ideas, and amusements into creators of personality and a social order. If our present institutional religion cannot function in this manner then a new form will arise to that end and it may not call itself religion at all.

If then organized Christianity is to help man to live creatively, it is not sufficient that it aid him to escape the forces of evil that oppose his every constructive effort, it must lead him to conquer them. The Barthians are right enough about the fatal pride and self-sufficiency of scientific intellectualism. They are just as wrong in proclaiming the utter helplessness of man, his absolute dependence upon a transcendent power—who is also a conception of the intellect made and proclaimed not entirely without pride. The facts continue to show, and moral development requires, interdependence between the person and the cosmos, between man and God, neither one being only the creation of the other, nor without the other capable of realization. Immanence and transcendence are not after all mutually exclusive.

The religion that brings salvation to modern man will help him to understand and develop the moral aspect of the universe even as science aids him to do that with its physical aspect. Then he will be able to direct life creatively instead of toward destruction, no matter how many times he stands baffled and ignorant, acknowledging his limitations and confessing his failure. At present most of our intellectuals perceive as little as the masses the nature and course of the forces that are undermining industrial society and piling up the chances of disaster for their children.

The preliminary condition of cure for the sickness of the acquisitive society—of which the United States is the climactic development just as Rome was the culmination of the great military empires—is that the prevailing pride and self-righteousness give way to an awareness of the premonitory symptoms and to some coöperative action against them. The efficacy of any program depends upon identification of the dominant causes of the disease, upon recognition of the fact that the acquisitive society is sick because it is acquisitive, because its attitude toward the cosmos is possessive rather than creative. To be effective this must be accompanied by a perception of the necessity of achieving a harmonized economic life, both between the classes and the nations. As Reinhold Niebuhr has emphasized, modern man is not whole in his own life because there is no solidarity in the common life; he cannot achieve the organic unity which the machine presupposes because while it unites him mechanically with a larger world it sunders him spiritually from his fellows. Because its bonds are impersonal and being used primarily for money-making, it sets the interests of one section against those of another.

Equally necessary to spiritual health and vigor is the recovery of some sense of the organic unity of life and culture. Now its various aspects are warring against each other—the practical needs against the intellectual, æsthetic, and spiritual—because commercialism has divided them. Such unity of life as belonged to simpler societies has been lost because economic pursuits have been put under the domain of the acquisitive spirit, subject to a morality different from that of art, science, or religion. The impetus of the machine added to the prestige and power of money-making has given the immediate and practical necessities of life a double ascendancy over its long-time imponderable values, and the house of civilization is thus divided against itself.

If it can be led to realize such organic unity as is possible to human life, the machine age will get some sense of direction to replace its present confusion and its distrust of purpose and ideals. Our generation has achieved its loss of direction largely through its inherited reliance upon the automatically beneficent outworkings of self-interest. Much of the contradiction in our political policies, for instance the increasing collectivism in behalf of profit seekers alongside the vociferous demand that the government refrain from interfering with business, is due to the survival of this eighteenth century belief. It is undoubtedly partly responsible for the naïve confidence of many preachers that our political and economic life will be saved merely by putting good men into executive positions. In the long run self-interest can never work out an intelligent social policy, no matter how much it is shown inevitable consequences, because it is inhibited from taking the risks involved in necessary change.

The other factor in keeping this generation without any conscious goal is the influence of the laboratory method and the philosophy that has developed around it. Under these influences we go from situation to situation, learning from each but with no sense of continuity or direction. What more then are we than opportunists? It is a curious turn of our intellectual life which deprives the generation that knows most of history and the rest of the world of any sense of social creativity. Here the Communists clearly have the advantage for they know what kind of world they want. Whereas our American liberals, religious and otherwise, seem to know only that they want to learn from the next experience, and some of them are as afraid of a purpose as medievalists were of the devil. Yet history shows that even a mistaken purpose may move the common life further forward than can those who know not where they are going. It is significant, however, that Dewey himself has said in the matter of war that next steps which are only refinements of the war making process are worse than nothing, because they are next steps in the wrong direction. This means that at least we must have enough sense of direction to know that we want to get away from war. And if war, then also some other equally menacing evils.

Thus the unconscious demand made upon religion by the modern man, all unaware of his need, is that it should help this wandering generation to fashion a goal for itself, should lead it to a creative consciousness of its organic possibilities, a dynamic awareness of present deficiencies. Religion has a twofold function for society as for the individual—to produce repentance accompanied by the power to forsake and overcome evil; to develop ideals along with the capacity to pursue and achieve them. In this twofold task it uses jointly the factual method of science and the imaginative insight of poetry. Concrete situations show the consequences of war, economic inequality and class division, along with the necessity of moving away from them. The vision of the ideal reveals the faint form of a warless world, a just and fraternal commonwealth, whose outline becomes clearer as man moves toward it by experimentation based on an increased understanding of past experience. It is by the power of the ideal that religion can encourage him to that creative effort in remaking his own life and fashioning the Great Society in which alone the modern man can harmonize the various aspects of his being and his culture and find some organic relationship to the universe.

A religion that does this will be something more than a *Preface to Morals* that unwittingly ends ethical development by leaving the good man a disinterested spectator of the drama of life. It will sustain him as a creative participant in the common struggle, renewing his hope and courage in times of defeat and increasing his enjoyment of its lighter interludes, because it gives him the consciousness of being allied with all that is timeless in continually diminishing its tragic catastrophes.

If Protestant Christianity is to become such a religion it must needs escape from the bonds of its traditional individualism and become conscious of its social value and mission. It must, as Freemantle urged a generation ago, take "the world as the subject of redemption" and understand what Ross a little later tried to teach it, the social nature of sin. Then it may be able to keep the growing awareness of his habitat by the modern man from becoming sterile sophistication and help it to become the creative intelligence that he needs. Early Protestantism helped to make it inevitable that the democratic individualism which supplanted the centralized and graded authority of the medieval world should in its turn gather Dead Sea fruit, by reinforcing the economic virtues without recognizing that they had been grafted on to the root of all evil. If modern Protestantism should likewise by its social service strengthen the collectivism of the machine age without perceiving where and how it is class dominated and mechanistic, without striving to transform it into a spiritual unity of coöperative effort for the development of all, its last state will indeed be much worse than its first. To avoid such an ending it must acquire on a larger and truer scale that sense of the civic nature of religion which possessed Greece in the days of her glory and distinguishes the faith of the Hebrews. But this must now be cast in the form of a continuous, humble, and repenting search for corporate salvation. The saving of civilization must be as prominent in the consciousness of modern religion as the saving of the soul was in the days when the world of the individual was replacing that of an interlocking feudal structure.

This means that it is the business of the churches to-day to know and to teach in what such a salvation consists. How can religion prevent the United States from developing into another parasitic empire, perishing in due time from the corruption of its luxury and power, unless it understands the nature of the forces that are making for decay, unless it knows the road that leads away from destruction, and the goal toward which man must strive? How can it help this broken, chaotic world and the mutilated, maladjusted personalities who inhabit it toward wholeness unless it realizes that human nature is more than the individual. American Protestantism is imperatively summoned to free itself from the absorption in the individual which has misled our psychology, and from the delusion that the common welfare is developed by the enlargement of personal self-interest which has deceived our classical economics. The ecclesiastical corollary is a doctrine of personal redemption in terms of self-gratification, followed by an assurance of salvation for society by the aura emanating from men who are good according to the standards of conventional religion. There are as few results to support this belief in the one field as in the other. In the easy calculation the overpowering effect of social institutions has been ignored. It is remarkable to see how liberals are confused by this hangover from the philosophic individualism of the eighteenth century. Why for example should the climax of Lippmann's *Preface to Morals,* after a diagnosis of a social situation and a glimpse at the Great Society in the making, be the disinterested individual? Why should liberal preachers keep repeating that we are to save modern society according to the method of Jesus by changing individual lives, regardless of the fact that Jesus never conceived of the individual apart from the community as moderns do, and of the fact that he was not facing a responsibility for the organization of society as we are?

In the kind of world in which we find ourselves a religion that is to help man into creative living must perceive and aid the increasingly organic relationship between the individual and society, must be aware of the social nature of the self, and all of its teaching and program must root in this knowledge. Society and the individual being inseparably bound together, religion cannot save either without the other, nor will the salvation of either follow automatically upon that of the other. What religion can do for the world is determined by what it can do for the person, and what it can do for the person is likewise limited by what it is able to do for society.

Unless it can progressively redeem the corporate life from its sins, religion cannot even keep the individual from the evil that is in the world. How much of holiness has it gained by keeping him from the carnal sins if the graces of the spirit are prevented by the conditions of associated living? How can it keep him pure in heart if the acquisitive society continually incites him to the love of riches and to covetousness? How can it enable him to enjoy the peaceable fruits of righteousness if his country orders him to bomb villages or cities? How can it inspire him to love his enemy if those in authority are determined that he shall hate him? How can he love his neighbor as himself if business causes him to use that neighbor—here or across the seas—as a serf laboring to supply his creature comforts? It is too late in the day for religion to proclaim an ethic of abstract personal virtues. To be anything more than an escape from surrounding iniquity these virtues must be translated into terms of current situations. The conscientious objector is justified against the society from which he rebels only when he cares more about the saving of mankind than his own soul. The modern man can find healing and wholeness, can become at home in the universe, only as he is conscious of working out an ethical salvation in coöperation with his community and with the rest of mankind.

3. WHICH KIND OF RELIGION?

When we ask which of the movements now claiming the interest and choice of the American churches show promise of meeting the joint needs of our corporate life and the modern man, both the revival of theology and of worship largely eliminate themselves from consideration. The larger section of each of these movements proclaims itself a return from the false path of the social gospel to the highway of spiritual religion, announces itself as substituting contact with the eternal for interest in current affairs. Taken at their own valuation, they are reaction, whatever the worth of that may be.

For the minority in these movements who assume that the ethical fruits of religion will inevitably follow a more vital interest in God through theology or worship, history has some warnings. The impotence of Scholasticism, the sterility of Unitarianism, are sufficient evidence that an intellectual interest in the problem of God has no inherent ethical power. There is likewise no warrant for thinking that philosophic humanism can avert the decay of capitalistic industrialism any more than Stoicism could that of the Roman Empire. On the other hand, the rise of the priestly cult following the reforming zeal of a prophetic group was the same in Israel as in Egypt. The priests provided no check, but in the end a stimulus, for moral decay. It is while the theological revival and the liturgical renaissance have been replacing the social movement in our religion that the moral evils which threaten our American life have risen to their greatest height.

If theology is primarily concerned with the cosmic problem, then its advocates have to reckon with the evidence summed up by Haydon in *The Quest of the Ages* to show that the gods are compensations for man's failure to achieve a satisfactory life here. There is, however, another chapter in the record. When ethical experience leads to discovery and rediscovery of an ethical God, then theology aids man in the moral struggle. But this is to make the human aspect of God secondary to the cosmic. Absorption in the cosmic problem provides for the rational temperament the same consolation in a decaying social order that ritual provides for the æsthetically inclined or revivalism for those of coarser emotions. It is another way of escape. Its appearance is admission of social defeat. It may then, like Stoicism, help its disciples to stand manfully, a heartening spectacle in a decaying world. But has American life reached that point? Are we already without the vigor to create and discover?

The tendency to withdrawal from the fighting front of man's struggle for a new race and a new world can be seen at both ends of the present interest in theology. At one extreme the Barthians tell us, with the authority of an absolute revelation, there is no way from man to God but only a way from God to man. At the other end the Humanists tell us there is no way from God to man because there is no God but only an indifferent cosmic energy. Meanwhile we may observe increasing contacts between the life of the ages and that of man, between the eternal power and human effort. Which aspect appears first in these connections varies according to temperament. The facts show that some men get an experience of an ethical God through human relations and effort, while others get into ethical human relations through the urge of a timeless imperative, conceived in terms of personality.

A theology that sunders man from the cosmos either in helplessness or independence, that fails to urge him to create continually anew himself and the world in which he lives, cannot meet the present need. It is not enough for theology to seek the nature of the eternal; its business is to find the relationship between the eternal and the now, between the ceaseless energy and the present striving. Its only chance of vitality and service in the age of science is to make the problem of sin and salvation—that is the moral need of man—its first and main business. Its concern with the nature of the universe will be secondary and at the points of its bearing upon the moral will of man. Inquiry into the other aspects of the cosmos belongs to science and philosophy, whose results must then receive moral assessment at the hands of religion. Theology will not connect the modern man with an ethical God until it realizes that his need for a cosmic faith is subordinate to his need for right and true living—that is right according to the concensus of his fellows in all time, and true according to the observations of science. What else is God for? What other is God than the exhaustless truth, the eternal righteousness, the everlasting love?

Those advocates of the present cult of beauty in worship who hold that it may lead to, as well as proceed from, the creative vitality of ethical experience will do well to analyze recent events in Russia. There a preëminently sensuous religion became not merely the bulwark of the established order but the inciter of repression. When Lenin thought of the church, what filled his mind was the sight of the priest on the scaffold blessing the executioner of his rebel brother. If it accepts the established order, a religion whose chief concern is ceremony naturally provides the ritual for the state as well as for the great events of personal life, blesses and sanctions its crowns and guns, its poison gas, prisons, scaffolds, and death chambers. In a corrupting and dying order, such a religion becomes naturally the accomplice of corruption and the tool of tyranny.

The only chance in such times of putting beauty in religion on the side of ethical advance is to make its ritual an emotional stimulus for the new order instead of an opiate for the endurance of the old. Here is the problem for the lovers of beauty in worship. It is more than a question of whether traditional forms of worship which are the product of a finished order and of vested institutional interests can be transferred to the forces that are breaking these up and making a new world; it is the deeper issue of the relation of timeless forces to temporary circumstances, the connection of the mood of abstraction with the daily struggle against current evil.

The Socialist wing of the Anglo-Catholics has gone the farthest in solving this problem. But they are a minority wing and in this country it is the Protestant wing of the Episcopalians which is socially minded. This goes to show that instead of æsthetic religion producing a type of social revolutionary, it is the passion for social transformation which is using the æsthetic interest for its purposes. When we observe the divergent purposes for which such antagonistic religious movements as the Roman Church and Russian Communism use dramatic ceremonial, it does not appear that the æsthetic interest in religion has any ethical content in its own right.

Anglo-Catholic Socialists affirm that it is their religious philosophy that makes them seek the transformation of the social order. If it is, then they have either performed the miracle of making sacramentarianism ethical or else they have unconsciously abandoned it, as for instance

[84]

when Conrad Noel says that the priest is not the mediator of God to the people but the representative of the people before God. It is an obvious historical fact that the sacramentarianism which usually accompanies ritual makes for a magical rather than an ethical religion, and with that peril its devotees have always to reckon. Indeed, the choice before American Protestantism at this hour as to which aspect of religion it will develop might almost be stated as the choice between an ethical and a magical religion. At least it is between the enlargement of the ethical or the magical elements in religion. For one rises always at the expense of the other. High church and revival tabernacle alike offer a magical salvation.

The essence of magic, whether expressed by incantations, charms, sorcery, or sacraments, is the invocation by man of powers other than his own skill or knowledge to do for him the things he is too ignorant or lazy or cowardly to do for himself. An ethical religion seeks to eliminate magic but seldom succeeds in doing more than minimize it. Its most superstitious forms are gone but it is still with us in certain ceremonies of even the more liberal churches. It is hard enough to erase ignorance from the creeds; it is still more difficult to exorcise superstition from the rituals. Magic may even be seen in the reliance upon phrases by antireligionist revolutionaries—those mighty words that summon irresistible forces to open the new day. To those who believe that all of life can be reduced to, and operated by scientific formula any use of faith is magical. So also is their faith in science. To give the ethical precedence over the magical does not reduce us to a world of purely human action, nor confine us to that which can be seen, measured, or weighed. There remain the imponderables. The question is how and for what may man seek to use the unseen.

A magical religion helps man to be lazy and selfish and to remain in ignorance. It keeps him depending upon the forces of the unseen world to aid him to get his food when he ought to be improving his own ways of providing it. It waves incense with incantations around the disease-stricken or insect-infested wheat field when it should be spraying with chemicals. This kind of magic disappears with the coming of science; but a magical religion is also used to keep in power the medicine man and the priest with their allies—the kings, nobles, and property owners. It becomes an appurtenance of privilege, a force to keep the people content and to be invoked against rebellion. Thus an other-worldly religion is in reality tremendously this-worldly, it maintains a wrong world instead of changing it into a right one. And this use of magic does not disappear with science. Whatever quarrel science may have with the use of magic for practical purposes, or for preventing inquiry into the nature of man or the universe, it seems to have none with its use to maintain or tolerate an unethical situation in the common life.

True, a magical religion can be used behind the desire to change the world, as a matter of fact has been so used on occasion, as it was in some of the ancient slave revolts. But thereafter, if it lives, it becomes an ethical religion as it did with the Hebrews. Generally, however, it fits in with the plans and purposes of the rulers of this world, who control its administration. To-day they offer no opposition to the development of the cosmic or æsthetic aspects of religion—so far its freedom is guaranteed—it is its ethical development that is objected to. It is, therefore, a foregone conclusion that if Protestantism turns back again toward the mysteries it will abandon the attempt to change the organized world and will accept a position subordinate to its principalities and powers. It will become a cheap edition of Rome, without any chance to acquire the authority that ancient church long enjoyed but cannot hold in the age of science. If Protestantism decides to exercise the prophetic function and develop the ethical elements in its religion, using theology and worship to continually improve the private and public life of man and calling both philosophy and science to aid in this endeavor, it is in for a stiff fight, within and without.

Religion becomes ethical by enlarging human fellowship, and the justice upon which it depends, as the condition of man's knowledge of and harmony with the eternal. By the same token, an ethical religion opposes injustice and special privilege and seeks to abolish them. It is for aid in this undertaking that it invokes the forces of the unseen world. It is, therefore, in no bondage to immoral deities, nor does it seek to use its ethical God for its own advantage. Just as true science uses the resources of the universe for the practical help of man in common, so does ethical religion use them for his moral development. There is no deeper treachery to man, no surer destruction of God, than the use of an ethical deity for selfish purposes. It is some evidence that there is a moral aspect to the universe and more for the moral capacity of man, that while this has been done often enough, it has never gone long without challenge from within the ranks of religion. When an ethical concept of deity is once reached, it continually asserts and vindicates itself in the demand for the purification and enlargement of ethical experience.

From the stupendous self-deception and betrayal of denying and destroying its own god religion is saved only when
it never seeks to invoke the unseen world for that which
man can do for himself and never for any interest less than
the whole of human welfare. This requirement puts sacrifice at the core of an ethical religion, not the sacrifice of
human beings on the altars of inhuman gods nor that of
the deity for the worshipper, but the sacrifice of God and
man together in the common cause of the ethical development of life—the just for the unjust, the loving for the
brutal—and thereby the achievement of fellowship instead
of self-righteousness.

On the other hand the tendency of religion to revert to
magic is accelerated by a theology which pictures God as
doing everything for man as much as it is by a ritualistic,
sacramentarian form of worship. Beyond doubt its defeat
by the World War revealed the inadequacy of liberal
Protestantism. But therefore to turn again to God to do
for us that which we can do for ourselves is to invite a
worse disaster through the weakening of our moral initiative and energy. This is as much a resurgence of the primitive as was the war itself. What modern man, religious,
irreligious, or antireligious, needs quickly and sharply to
realize is that neither God nor science have any magical
power. For the alternating modern moods of pride and
despair a more effective antidote than absolute dependence upon God is needed. The true remedy will be found
in that mutualism between man and God, between the
temporary and the timeless aspects of the universe, which
we know by experience to be the best working and most
satisfying arrangement between human beings.

It appears then that if our choice of which aspect of

religion is now to be developed is determined by capacity to minister to the need of the hour it will be an ethical religion that we will seek. The functional test gives us the same answer as that reached by examination of the historic consequences of acceding to the demand of the powers of this world for submission. The only kind of religion which can meet man's present need is the only kind that can save itself from subordination to the temporary aspects of life—that is a religion whose God is ethical, whose salvation is progressively moral, whose worship is designed to aid the continuous transformation of life into nobler forms. Can any other save civilization from decay, continue the personal quest for holiness, or meet the demands and secure the coöperation of the spirit of science?

4. SIGNS OF PROMISE

When we look for signs of the development of this type of religion, at once there come into view the protests made by American churches against the evils that threaten industrial society accompanied by serious educational effort to set forth their nature, causes, and consequences and to participate in concrete measures to check their development. They have proclaimed war to be the greatest collective crime of humanity, they have denounced imperialist policies, the appeal of their preachers against denial of constitutional rights and miscarriage of justice in the industrial conflict is stronger than that from any other vocational group. This constitutes no mean record. Its effectiveness cannot be measured until another generation shows whether religious education can produce the type of religious person who is able, because he understands it better than those who went before him, to withstand and change the world that ever threatens the life of the spirit.

Taking the religious offensive against the forces of evil that imperil the future of civilization as it stands to-day, those who have been leading it would be the first to admit and lament its inadequacy. It is in all the churches a minority movement little affecting the judgments and conduct of the great bulk of the membership. It is viewed by ecclesiastical authorities as a departmental activity—a form of good works, an attachment to the religious life—rather than an essential and imperative expression of religion. When set against what remains to be accomplished if civilization is to be saved and modern man to find a working religion, it appears smaller still.

This can be most easily seen in the case of the widest and most thoroughgoing of the efforts to develop the ethical aspect of religion—the demand of the churches for a warless world, for limitation of armaments and military training, and their support of legislation to these ends. In this matter the churches have moved away from vague, pious sentimentality toward practical concreteness. Their main reliance has been upon the automatic effect of a realization of the consequences of war. Here they follow the scientific method, the shaping of action according to observed results. But this procedure is sharply checked when it runs into inherited traditions and the emotions they evoke, as for instance in the spread of information concerning methods of birth control. So we go on with preparedness in aircraft and poison gas though we know very well that chemical warfare means swift and whole-sale destruction for noncombatants and their cities. Nor is it likely that a pragmatic ethic alone will carry us over these intrenchments of passion and prejudice.

So powerful are the traditional ideas of patriotism, security, and defense when reinforced by the emotions they arouse that against them reason is powerless and the facts of no avail, especially when the war cult derives new vigor from the cult of money-making with its additional demand for security and defense by force. How powerful are those misdirected emotions and antiquated ideas may be seen from the case of the Quakers. The essence of their faith is confidence in the power of goodwill, and opposition to war has been their distinctive ethical standard. Yet there are Quakers to-day supporting a policy of defensive armaments. Small wonder then that politicians pursue the old illusions about security, that high school boys fall easy victim to the propaganda for military training, that church members are active against as well as for the Kellogg Pact.

In centering so much of their efforts for a warless world upon immediate steps, the leaders of the ethical movement in religion have not taken the measure of the innate tendencies of human society toward conflict and their acceleration by industrialism. What is more significant is they they seem not to have realized the peculiar capacities of their religion for the removal of these tendencies. Because the essence of religion is an emotional choice of values, no matter how much this may be supported or dictated by reason, its particular function is to enable man to direct his emotions constantly toward higher and wider ethical ends. If this process, instead of being validated by concern with next steps is supplanted by absorption in them, then the strength that religion has derived from science will be turned into weakness. Other organizations can and will plan campaigns against cruiser bills and military training and church members will act in and with them. But who else will make the people see that nationalism in the modern world is a mortal sin? Who else will enable them to understand that defense and security lie not in armaments but in just and mutual arrangements with the rest of the world? Who else will help them transfer the priceless quality of loyalty from the limited circle to a larger field, the emotions expended in local patriotism to the whole of humanity?

The realistic school of historians is hard at work debunking a flabby, sentimental patriotism and exposing the limitations of nationalism, but their attack is purely negative. If they work alone they produce cynical world weariness and the sense of futility. If the road into a new world order is to be built after they have blasted away some of the obstacles, religion will need to give a larger and more positive outlet to the emotions manifested in patriotism, a more constructive content to the ethical values involved in group loyalty. If all it is able to do is to echo the language of science and point to the consequences of war, its appeal is once again to fear and the militarist has the advantage of manifesting his courage. This he loses only when religion offers a moral substitute for war in the building of a new world with tools that are dangerous. When for this purpose it joins hands with science, uniting faith and reason, perception of factual consequences with aspiration for the ideal, extending the values approved by experience in smaller groupings to larger and larger areas, then progress is assured.

This is so obvious as to be almost trite, yet our current

church campaign gives more attention to the economic causes of war—which standing alone is much to its credit —than to the false ideas and misdirected emotions that support and respond to the propaganda for preparedness. Here and there a powerful voice in the pulpit speaks out against nationalism and declares that patriotism is not enough, but for the most part this attack is left to the labor and socialist movement which with its gospel of solidarity then takes on the aspect of religion. It is almost a commonplace among progressive preachers that the scale of loyalties runs from the family through the nation, to mankind. But this will have to be taught much more concretely and powerfully in and through the churches if the new nationalism is to be kept from making this country the enemy of mankind.

When we look at the relation of the American churches to imperialism—the twin of militarism—we find a different situation. Naturally enough, despite the protest against particular policies, there is no such recognition of its nature and consequences. One conditioning fact is that religion is institutionally related to imperialism as it is not to war. Its foreign missionary enterprise has both gone before and followed after the flag, has many times claimed and received protection from the state. The awakening Orient sees no separation between Western imperialism and Western missions. Not only has each helped the other, but they are both of them expressions of the aggressive nature of the Western peoples, though as antagonistic on other sides as children of the same parents often are. It is characteristic of modern missions that they carry a culture as well as a religion, and in some cases do not seem to know which is their primary purpose. They have renounced the Roman desire to make one church for all the world, and forsaken the Protestant ambition to spread one authoritative scripture, but the essence of imperialism is still there. When Oriental intellectuals protest against the cultural penetration of the West, it is the work of mission schools and colleges that they have in mind. Before religion can free the state from imperialistic ambitions it must first get rid of them itself.

This is what the newer missions have done. Its exponents have renounced the imperialistic urge that is behind the attempt to convert others to one's own faith and gather them into one's own denomination. They go to other lands not to bestow but to share. They seek not the subjection of other people to their religion or culture but the joint conquest of life as a mutual enterprise. When imperialism is thus eliminated from the heart and practice of the churches, they do not need the protection of the imperialist state. As a matter of fact minority groups of missionaries are now refusing it and the Boards themselves decline any longer to use the state to collect compensation for deaths, injuries, and losses. It is by themselves renouncing the idea of conquest that the churches can deliver their strongest blow against imperialism. When the spirit of mutualism entirely replaces that of aggression in the relation of organized religion to those of other faiths and of none, there will be ground for hope that it may also come to control the joint world of government and business, that resources and technical capacity may be considered mutual possessions to be jointly administered. Then they too will need no protection by armed forces, but only education in their proper use.

A similar need to make more ethical their own life

appears when we examine the record of the churches in relation to the recent repression of civil liberties. The challenging fact is the extent to which church attitudes follow rather than transcend the class lines of our economic structure. The denial of constitutional rights has been strongest in industrial communities. In notable instances, preachers have stood out against such injustice and lawlessness regardless of local economic interests. But in general, North and South, the churches divide on class lines in their attitude in the industrial conflict. The older middle class churches are usually against the strikers and indifferent to the denial of their civil rights, while the wage earners' churches naturally come ardently to their support. In the churches of mixed membership there is a split.

Thus the issue of civil liberties runs into that of class consciousness and class antagonism. In this particular ecclesiastical society follows the pattern of society in general. As income and property become concentrated and class division appears, the churches also divide into richer and poorer, and pastoral supply is necessarily determined on a money basis. The churches of small income get a certain kind of preacher. The preacher's progress in ecclesiastical preferment is marked by a progressive income scale. The early Christian churches were warned about letting the divisions of the world appear within their borders. Modern Christianity, particularly its ministry, still boasts itself a spiritual fraternity. But with what reality if it is dominated by the pecuniary standards of capitalistic industrialism?

It is a sign of hope that in various quarters a vigorous attempt is being made to remove and prevent the existing inequalities in preachers' incomes. But there still remains the underlying fact of increasing class division running through the whole life and polity of the churches. As in the world outside, control tends to concentrate in the hands of the upper income groups. This is as perilous for society as it is for the church. When religion becomes class conscious in response to the stratification of society, it accelerates the internecine warfare of the industrial age by throwing the most powerful sanctions behind it. The only religion that can save the world is one ethical enough to abolish class divisions in its own household, and intelligent enough to apply itself to the removal of their causes in the economic organization of society.

In the matter of the corruption that has disgraced our public life since the World War there appears a still sharper need of ethical transformation within the churches. They count in their membership not a few of the participants in this orgy of graft. Along with some who participated in the conspiracy of concealment for the crimes and others who obstructed their exposure, these persons are still in good and regular standing. Of those distinguished public men who kept dishonored silence when words of rebuke might have aroused the slumbering conscience of the nation not a few are lay leaders in their respective denominations, who are still proud to have produced and to be represented by them.

This is a different thing for the churches than producing exponents of militarism and imperialism. The standards of political honesty are known and approved. Yet organized religion appears unable to get them carried out in the lives of some of its most distinguished representatives. While the nation has been robbed, organized religion has not only been passing down the road unheeding;

it has given some aid and comfort to the bandits. The revival of interest in spiritual things that was heralded after the war has coincided with a bigger renaissance of corruption. Neither in its ordinary institutional manifestations nor in its newer tendencies has religion had sufficient ethical vitality to prevent this fouling of its own house.

The reasons are not hard to find. Such moral energy as the churches had put into politics went mostly into the prohibition movement. These honorable churchmen who were trying to hush up the infamy of their political associates, and to cry down the activities of those who were exposing it, were motivated most of all by a desire to protect the party. Their religion had never taught them the nature of loyalty. For them, as for the street gamin and the gangster, it was only sticking by your crowd. Sectarian religion has difficulty itself in learning the larger meaning of loyalty. Only as it continues to develop in its own life the morality of putting the whole always before the part can organized religion hope to teach that ethic in national politics and international relations.

The deeper cause of the failure of organized religion to produce a higher type of political morality in the person of its own laymen is the relation between politics and business. The grafters were brought up in a local political machine which expected to be used by business and to make business pay for it. From the pulpit and in young people's societies they heard about good citizenship and public service, but the practical course of politics was another matter. There you had to fight for what you got and could not be too particular in the choice of weapons. Underneath all was the grim fact of money-making as the dominant and determining activity of life. If business is run for profit it is inevitable that politics will be run for the same end. In both activities the line between honesty and graft, earned and easy money, is very thin and easily eliminated. Political corruption roots in the use of organized politics by the successful money-making interests exactly as they use natural resources and their fellow human beings for the same purpose. In a world where that is the accepted and laudable procedure, while the standards between the profit makers gradually grow higher—like honor among thieves, concerning the relations between the intrenched profit takers and the public they gradually decline. Do not our courts for the most part protect unearned income?

The manifest weakness of religion in preventing political dishonesty from developing within its own ranks is a sign of its ineffectiveness in assessing or opposing the cult of money-making. That cult also sustains our current developments of militarism, imperialism, and repression, yet even the social movement in the churches has dealt but little with it. The belief that the social well-being comes from the pursuit of individual advantage in the form of financial gain constitutes an unavoidable challenge to mortal combat to a religion which proclaims that a man's life consists not in the abundance of the things he possesses, which has historically ranked avarice among the deadly sins alongside murder and adultery. Failing to accept this challenge, religion itself becomes infected and degenerated by the sickness of the acquisitive society. It then proclaims success in money-making to be a sign of virtue and evidence of God's favor. It permits its adherents unchecked to prefer comfort to justice, so that naturally some of them come to choose it before honesty or loyalty to the national welfare. Then it offers them pardon without repentance or restitution, or holds out a promise of salvation and a hope of heaven that are dependent like profit upon the losses of others. Its moral qualities are also the economic virtues and these weaken and destroy the distinctive ethical values of its gospel. Thus the force that is able to save civilization from the decay that follows the pursuit of material wealth is turned into an accomplice in its destruction.

This cursory glance at the efforts of the churches to check the evils of modern life shows us a record in which need far outruns achievement. For this movement to fulfill its promise requires the support of religion as a whole. Theology and worship, instead of appearing as competitors of the ethical aspect of religion, will need to become its supporters. To overcome the prevailing vital and seductive faith in the omnipotence of money Christianity will need to muster all its forces. If it is to help man build the civilization, which so far he has attempted only to fail, it will have to recognize itself as potentially an ethical religion, and bend all its energies to develop its ethical capacities.

5. THE DOMINANT TREND

What is the possibility of this happening in American Protestantism? At present, for all its attempts at federated action and its movements toward unity, it is a bizarre pattern of differing sects, each of them originating in some particular emphasis on one of the aspects of religion—theology or ritual, church government or the conduct of life. Is there any sign of a dominant trend? Is there anything to indicate which of the interests—theological, liturgical, ethical—now agitating its leadership is likely to prevail?

In a rough characterization the early religion of New England may be set down as predominantly theological, with a strong practical emphasis which was drawn out by the necessity for community organization as well as by inherited reaction against the European manner of life and government. The formal separation of church and state was accompanied by the expectation that religion was to control the community life. Its power was to be moral not legal. The church was the center of the community, religious ideas controlled community regulations. The emphasis upon theology in due time occasioned the rise of Unitarianism, and the opening up of the West brought vast wealth and different human relations. In the face of the vital ethical questions thus raised, the issue between orthodox and heterodox was futile. Theology became sterile. Like Scholasticism it had compassed its limited world. It had reached a bounded system where there was nothing to do but go round and round. The expanding possibilities for religion were in the realm of human behavior, until science raised new issues for theology. Meantime the insatiable religious hunger of man was satisfied for a time by an emotional revivalism with a less rigid theology. It was a process repeated in a smaller field by the rise of Humanism recently among the Unitarians. But none of these movements came to grips with the basic economic issue where both religion and ethics find their final defeat or justification.

The early religion of the South and West was emotional and practical. Other stocks with their religious traditions and habits flowed in—the Cavalier strain was in the South and the Germans, the Irish, and the Scandinavians came to the Middle West. The work of subduing virgin soil into plantations and farms was not favorable to the development of either theology or liturgy. The words and works of religion took on something of the roughness of those of daily living. While the liturgical emphasis survived in the South as a class distinction, it did not develop. The prevailing tone became that of the Noncomformist sects. Revivalism was the dominant feature, with protracted meetings as its chief expression. Lacking the influence of the New England intellectualism that touched the early religious life of the Middle West, its attitudes on the ethical issues of slavery and liquor were determined more directly by class interest, Southern Protestanism to-day is naturally more obscurantist than the same type of religion in the North, more belligerent in defending the literal inspiration and verbal authority of Scripture. The theological interest is dominated by emotion not reason.

In harmony with the conditions of the frontier, revivalism became also the dominant feature of religion in the West. It submerged theology as it had liturgy in the South. Its moral offensive was against the carnal sins—licentiousness, drunkenness, brawling—and these were viewed as purely personal manifestations. The major ethical issue—the love of money—was likewise treated as a personal disposition; as an economic motivation, a social cult, it was ignored except for a few lone voices. Naturally enough preachers can now speculate on the stock market in good conscience. After the Civil War revivalism, devitalized by its lack of a social ethic, became more and more stereotyped and artificial. The churches,

CERTIFIED SEMINARY
LIBRARY
NEW YORK

like the nation, had split over slavery, and with them it was an ethical issue. The next challenge of the same sort was the rise of the money power, but its sun dawned imperceptibly upon the religious world. Even the political corruption that accompanied it apparently went unnoticed. Had not the party supported by the churches freed the slave? To suggest that the king could do wrong was moral treason. So a revivalism that was separated from the economic question, where the real ethical issue lay, became in the end commercialized as well as stereotyped, itself part and parcel of the predatory system of money-making from which it is the business of religion to save man even as it is his necessity to be saved.

In its later development American Protestantism has become predominantly institutional, with emphasis upon efficiency in doing good as the present expression of its continuous practical bent. Its evangelism operates now but feebly under forced draught. Its theology, until the revival of interest following the World War, has been secondary to concrete activities. Its moral energy has been expressed largely in the legalistic social reforms that are now getting it so cordially hated by certain sections of the population. It is mostly engaged in building ecclesiastical organizations which require most of the energy they produce for the turning of their own wheels. The original characteristic emphases of the denominations tend to disappear, save for a few small sects which find it increasingly difficult with each younger generation to preserve their type. Most of them grow or merge into larger groupings that minister to all types by combining the various aspects of religion after the manner of Roman Catholicism, so that the extremes meet under one ecclesi-

astical label. Thus, the Methodists now affect liturgy, the Congregationalists develop centralized administration, and the Quakers acquire ministers. As with political parties, the differences between the churches tend to disappear. This is not only for the same reason—that they follow rather than change the standardizing money culture of the age—but also because they are all adapting themselves to the new intellectual climate produced by the rise of science.

It will not be questioned that at the present moment the dominant trend in American Protestantism is toward institutionalism. Our denominations are on the way to become bigger and better machines. Their movement is mostly that of routine, which always inclines toward inertia, so that a religious journal calmly observes that one of the hardest problems of a preacher is to find something for his members to do. Recent developments in theology, worship, and social service are outside the interest of multitudes of church members, whose religion derives purely from tradition and proceeds entirely by custom. The constant complaint of younger preachers is that so much of their time and energy must be spent on institutional affairs. Indeed the trend toward mysticism and æstheticism is in part a revolt against the increasing dominance of routine.

The real conflict after all is not between the intellectual, emotional, and ethical aspects of religion. To view them competitively is disastrous because it divides the forces before the enemy who never sleeps—the world. The basic issue is whether the congeries of movements and tendencies that is Protestantism is to coalesce into another great religious institution, which will indeed make room for all the vital aspects of religion—will have due place for theology and worship and social service—but will subordinate them all to its own power and glory instead of coördinating them for the continuous regeneration of the soul and society of man regardless of what happens to itself.

The conflict between institutional and ethical religion is inherent, so much so that it is an open question whether an ethical religion can ever be carried forward except by recurring minority movements. The accession to power and wealth of the Protestant denominations puts before them a similar question to that so dramatically raised concerning the state by current developments in two countries as different as the United States and Russia—can a powerful institution ever be moral. In the inherent contradiction between power and ethical living, conjoined with the tendency toward repetitive routine, lies the explanation of the low vitality of organized religion, so pungently described by Lippmann in his *Prefare to Morals* and so pathetically concurred in by our evangelical leaders. The ethical potency of our churches does not measure up to their capacity any more than their intellectual leadership comes up to the intelligence of their leading preachers. Their general influence does not correspond to the quality of their effort. It is conceded that the movies and the newspapers mold the attitudes and behavior of the common people more than the pulpit and the church school. What passes for science is more influential with the youth of our universities than what is offered them as religion. The efforts of many able and devoted persons to alter this state of affairs are discounted by institutional routine. A considerable section of both clergy and laity respond both intellectually and emotionally to the challenge of an ethical religion, but institutionally the churches are not geared to pull that load.

The inevitable tendency toward uniformity that age brings to all human institutions has been accentuated in the American churches by the pressure of events in the business world. There combination and standardization are the order of the day. So organized religion also standardizes its activities, acquires efficiency methods and develops mergers. The familiar gibe at the practical incompetence of the preacher is hopelessly out of date. Our religious executives need have no inferiority complex before business men. Indeed, some of them could reverse the old taunt and say, "If my office were run like your business I would not last long." The denominations have reached the point where figures showing membership, income, and property count more than their meaning and cost in life. Churches are now mobilized like an army and preachers drilled like cadets in the goose step. For world service it is true, but that too becomes machine made and may find itself far away from the actual needs and perils of the world.

As the desire for bigness and mechanical perfection grows, it demands a higher price for its realization than the deadening "safety first" which is the guiding principle of all established institutions and vested interests. Harmony becomes a cult, so that he who disturbs it by raising critical questions is made to feel as comfortable as a pessimist in a Rotary meeting. Tolerance is now the note in progressive Christianity. Only Fundamentalists force issues. Liberals apparently have none that are imperative enough to be worth championing. They are mostly occupied in finding out how to agree. Some day, in the course of nature, a price will be named for harmony that is too high to pay, but for the moment the tendency is to seek unity no matter what the incompatibilities, to preserve a fictitious peace by silence concerning ethical differences that are vital. The immorality of some of our ecclesiastical alliances is just as gross and quite as disastrous to society as that of our bipartisan political plunder gangs.

The emphasis upon unity in religion is again one of the signs of a closing era, when institutions have come to the climax of their capacities and new forms are due to appear. Those in our churches who are afraid to have them face the major ethical issues of the day because of the inevitable division of forces that will follow are in reality afraid of the process of life. Reproduction is by division as well as amalgamation. When the churches cannot take hold of the divisive issues it means that they have lost creative capacity, that organized religion has become senile, that its vital function must be assumed by a new grouping.

It is customary among current writers to attribute the rise of the divisive ethical questions now before modern society to the emergence of the machine. That is a half truth, or perhaps only a quarter. Behind these issues there is also: the rise of the money power through control of the machine, and the natural and human resources which feed it, by a small section of the population; the new intelligence due to the spread of the method and results of science; the rise of the working class with increasing determination and growing power to achieve the new world of which the machine gives promise. Protestantism is the religious expression of a somewhat similar conjunction of social forces that put in power the trading class whose needs it has served and by whom it is controlled. If now it cannot adapt itself to the needs of the working class and aid in making the kind of world that the common interests of humanity require, it will in due course give way to another type of religion.

Here there comes into view again the question of whether a vital attempt at an ethical religion must always be a minority movement which in time is turned into an institution that develops unmoral and then immoral aspects, so that the search for higher forms of life has to be carried on by another secession. This is the course traced by Richard Niebuhr in his *Social Sources of Denominationalism* and it holds true for a much wider area of history. Whether or not it is the only course depends upon what existing institutions can do to solve the problem of authority in its relation to growth. In that matter Roman Catholicism has taken one attitude and its strikingly similar, yet vitally different enemy, Russian Communism, has taken another. Each has at certain points an infallible and inflexible authority that seeks to preserve unchanged a dogma and an institution which it believes best adapted to the needs of mankind. But Communism thinks it can avoid the progressive anemia of institutionalism by making the bureaucracy which is unavoidable in a complex society continuously responsive to the masses of the people. This is just what the parliamentary system promised and failed to achieve. If the machinery of a social institution enables popular control and is sufficiently flexible to record the desire for change, then the test of whether it checks rather than encourages the moral growth of those connected with it turns upon its educational system. The question is whether or not this shapes the desires of the people in the interests of the bureaucracy by what it refuses or fails to discuss.

At this point progressive Protestantism in the United States, with its emphasis upon complete freedom of inquiry, offers an interesting contrast to both Catholicism and Communism. The possibility of its freeing itself from the disease of institutionalism turns upon the fact that our bigger and better religious machines are being manned in large degree by the younger and more liberal men who are under the influence of the newer methods in religious education. So it has come about that our standardized denominational procedure includes a considerable curriculum for discussing the ethical meaning and duties of the Christian religion. If this can bear fruit not only in those practical activities to which our climate inclines us but also in constant self-criticism and improvement, then American Protestantism may contribute something toward the discovery of how to rejuvenate the institutions of society without the shock and waste of sudden and violent revolution. The condition of maintaining the process of revaluation in either church or state is, of course, a thoroughgoing acceptance of the functional point of view with its insistence that all social institutions exist for something bigger than themselves—the well-being of humanity as a whole.

6. PHYSICIAN HEAL THYSELF!

For organized religion to follow this course involves some risk for those in charge of it. It requires that preachers take the same chance of unemployment and blacklist that attends those wage earners in certain industries who are active in the labor movement. Also, what is harder, it requires them to take the risk of poverty and starvation for the institution which is the pride of their lives, which for all its apostasies has kept truth alive, has nurtured the prophets even while it stoned them and garlanded their tombs. If our religious institutions are to survive these risks it means that those who provide their financial support must see the need of their revaluing function and be willing to pay for it even when it hurts. Free churches have more chance of developing this virtue than those whose revenues are derived from the state. But when they begin to revalue political and economic institutions, those in any kind of church will meet the charge of treason added to that of Bolshevism.

But, because it is the custodian of the ethic of service and sacrifice, organized religion is under peculiar obligation to attempt this path. Its high calling is to develop and test values as well as conserve them. Only by asserting its independence of the economic and political forces by which it is nourished and protected can it bring to them that power of ethical growth which is their only salvation from decay. The development of the ethical religion that civilization needs to save it from the evils now threatening its life depends upon an ethical view and practice of the church. If organized religion is to save the world it must be able to save itself, and it can only save itself by being willing to lose its own life in the attempt to save the world.

It appears then that the same measures will free religion from the deadly embrace of institutionalism which enable it to resist the seducing stimulus of emotionalism or the chilling touch of intellectualism. These dangers can only be avoided by the development of its ethical aspect as the regulating factor which, by coördinating them in a common aim, keeps the other elements from developing to excess, prevents them from weakening each other in prideful competition or menacing human freedom and happiness in blind ambition. An ethical purpose keeps theology engaged with life and not with esoteric speculation, makes emotion a dynamic for the conquest of life not an escape from the battle into mystic peace or liturgic exaltation, saves institutions from becoming tombs by keeping them in use as tools. Without the dominance of an ethical purpose the machinery, the intellectual pursuits, and the worship of religion all become means for the appropriation of God to personal or class ends, even for economic purposes, as in prayers and thanksgiving for prosperity for ourselves. Then religion becomes self-deceiving. It leads men to believe that God is on their side when they are only rationalizing their desires as his, whereas the condition of alliance with the eternal will is the constant effort to find out how much justice and fellowship can be realized in any given situation. When religion becomes self-centered civilization has no chance of avoiding disaster. It must gradually perish of old age or tear itself apart in revolutionary conflict. Where can it get the spirit of sacrifice which is its only means of renewal if religion has it not?

But when the institutions of religion are self-sacrificingly functional—that is when they operate solely for the preservation and development of those values which experience has proved most necessary to the common life and not for its control by any class, priestly, military, or economic—then it can influence the state and the economic order to take the same high ground. Then also, it ceases to dispute with them for the control of society and coördinates with them on a functional basis. Thus it may keep them from developing their man-devouring tendencies, prevent them from becoming false gods and demanding human sacrifice. Its one demand is that they shall work with it in the finding and furthering of those aims in which the achievement of personality consists, to whose pursuit all social institutions must be subordinate and in whose realization they alone are justified. In like manner it seeks spiritual alliance with art and science in the common purpose of aiding men to enjoy life not possessively but creatively through the continuous development of higher forms of ethical living.

Thus to develop the ethical aspect of religion is not to reduce it to a system of ethics or to a set of ethical principles. Still less does it produce the legalism of the Scribes, the self-righteousness of the Pharisees, or the static complacency of old China. The former destroyed an ethical religion by reducing it to a set of maxims or a code of legal trivialities; the latter limited an ethical religion by trying to bound life with a circle so that there was nothing to do but walk around inside it. Religion can escape both fates by treating ethical development as a continuous process of experience, by viewing it as the continued unfolding of the possibilities of human living, by using it as the key to the solution of the riddle of the universe, following it as the path that leads from man to God and from God to man. Then its ethics will be dynamic not static, experimental not dogmatic, neither separated from the discoveries of the past nor shut off from the exploration of the future.

There is a vital difference between an ethical religion and a system of ethics. The latter usually means a process of thought or a compilation of rules. It is philosophy where it is not regulation, both of them made mostly from the materials of the past and the older they get having less and less use for Utopia, without which the universe is dead. Religion, however, has the poetic element of creative imagination. Wherever it is vital it is never without the apocalyptic vision. It announces a new heaven and a new earth. It proclaims the illimitable possibilities. At its best it offers man a future to be made not merely waited for, a future to be lived with in its promise, its hope, and its continual coming. By this touch of immortality religion saves ethics from both intellectualism and legalism, joins the moral struggle of man with the eternal power.

Proceeding on this ground, an ethical religion provides a way through two problems which perennially trouble man. The old antithesis between faith and works is removed as man works out—by faith in and with an ethical God, himself, and his fellows—his salvation, seeking it not for himself alone but for the whole human race. The self-righteousness of formal good works, or meritorious deeds and qualities, is not replaced by a mystical substitutionary righteousness but by an active participation in the moral struggle, a concrete realization of redemption in the continuous improvement of human life.

Likewise an ethical religion opens up a road for an unceasing attack upon the problem of evil. It knows the bitterness of living with the body of this death, the necessity and joy of finding release from it. But it does not find that release in a theological formula any more than in the magic words of a priest. Nor does it turn the matter over to the psychopath, though it needs and uses his help at times. It knows with Barth and with Paul that our goodness is not adequate to remove the evil that is in the world, but it also knows that sin exists in particular attitudes and deeds of man. It, therefore, is not content merely to talk or think or feel about sin in general, but by analysis of current situations it shows men what they must hate and quit and destroy. It does not stop with the delinquencies of abnormal and maladjusted personality but goes on to the basic sins of organized society—its lust and greed, its luxury and power and strife.

The question then is whether as the American Protestant churches become conscious of themselves in relation to organized society, that self-consciousness will take the form of viewing themselves as agencies for the development of an ethical religion. This question is as vital for industrial civilization as it is for religion. If the ethical aspect of religion does not develop, then as civilization grows old there is no saving salt to keep it from decay. Its gods are many, all of them tolerated, and nothing more. Religious faith, like any other enthusiasm, is found rather amusing. The perennial talk about a revival of religion—meaning its magical forms and its mystic words —is futile. What chance in a scientific, acquisitive age has a magical, a mystic, an æsthetic, or a purely cosmic religion to be anything else than a feeble defense of outworn privilege, regarded with a polite cynicism by those who seek in vain thus to use it. The only religious awakening that can meet the need of modern man is one that will save him from frustration and futility by urging and holding him to the difficult task of making the civilization of which he now so glibly and deceptively talks. How else can he avoid the sins that have destroyed the works of his ancestors? How else can he come to terms with the cosmic problem? If he finds out how to live he will know, as always, how to die; and the universe, even though it be centered beyond the stars and only partly understood, will nevertheless find a sufficient vindication in his own creative struggle.

CHAPTER III

THE ETHICAL VALUE OF THE RELIGION OF JESUS

1. BY COMMON CONSENT

IN estimating the possibility of American Protestantism developing into an ethical religion, either alone or in company with kindred movements elsewhere, it is necessary to assess the values raised by the demand now being made within its own ranks that it become the religion of Jesus instead of a religion about him. This demand is the culmination of the "Back to Jesus" movement which was occasioned by the new light thrown upon the Galilean by modern biblical research. It now urges that his way of life be substituted for that of civilization, and that organized religion accept this as its task. Thus there has come to this generation a sense of the difference between the words of Jesus and those of the church, between his ways and those of society, similar to that which came to the common people of feudal England when they first heard the gospels in the vernacular.

While plenty of preachers and church members still do Jesus the injustice and bring him the discredit of assuming that Christianity is his religion, the informed know that it is a composite into which there went first the theology of Paul and then some things from the mystery cults and philosophies of Greece and others from the hero worship and imperial organization of Rome. As this is understood it gives still another aspect to the choice now before the churches. Which will they decide to develop, traditional Christianity or the religion of Jesus? If they take his religion how will it affect the other choices that now confront them? What then will be their attitude toward the power and the glory of this world? Which aspect of religion will become central—theology, worship, or the improvement of life?

To put the question this way is not to beg it by giving the word of Jesus an authority he never claimed for himself. He is reported to have urged his followers to go on discovering truth, yet the churches have so often used him as though his was the last word that many who to-day properly revolt against the authoritarian method are thereby prevented from perceiving the values that belong to his religion. To recognize that Paul gave Christianity a direction different at points from that of Jesus, to be aware that it is a composite, is not thereby to assume that either developments are wrong. The values are yet to be proved. Certainly the teacher who proclaimed that ethical results were the proof of religious professions would be willing to stand or fall by the functional test. Whether the elements in our organized religion that are accretions to or deviations from the religion of Jesus should be kept depends upon their worth to modern life. Whether or not we should now develop his faith and manner of life depends upon whether it has the capacity to meet the needs of the world to-day and to-morrow, not at all upon the fact that it was his. The last name in the world that men have a right to use as though it had imperial or magical power is that of the carpenter of Nazareth. Yet

Protestantism has carried over both uses from older forms of Christianity—particularly in its more sentimental hymns.

Nevertheless, so powerful and so generally recognized is the distinguishing characteristic of the religion of Jesus, that it manifests itself even when men use his name as though it had magic power. It is for example not uncommon for those who become aware that our civilization is developing symptoms of the disease that has proved fatal to others to say that only Jesus can save us. How often was it said in the dark days of the war by those who were terrified at the sudden sight of what lies beneath our culture. In the moral reaction that followed the great conflict it has become almost a commonplace for liberal preachers to declare that nothing but the principles of Jesus can save civilization. It has become almost a professional formula, and there is plainly a vestige of magic in it. What virtue then has the Galilean that in the age of science men should call upon him when the house of civilization is falling about their heads?

When men, within and without the churches, thus invoke the name of Jesus it is obvious that they recognize something different about his religion than they see or practice in that of the creeds. From conventional Christianity they do not—even its administrators—so confidently expect salvation for mankind. Here is something deeper than an intellectual perception of the discrepancy between what Jesus said and did in the brief record of him that remains and a good deal that his professed followers say and do in his name. The vitality of his religion is manifesting itself against that of the churches. The recurrent resurrection of Jesus is one of the challenging facts of history. Over and over again church and state together crucify him and proclaim him dead; over and over again he reappears to challenge them to new ways. The nature of this vitality is apparent in the paradoxical fact that even when men use his name magically it is with ethical significance. When they say that the principles of Jesus can save civilization they recognize that the morality of the Sermon on the Mount is higher than that of organized society, they are talking the language of an ethical not a theological or liturgical religion.

Similar testimony concerning the characteristic to which the religion of Jesus owes its vitality comes consistently from those outside the ranks of ecclesiastical Christianity. They are free from its prepossessions. To them the Christ of the churches does not speak, only the Jesus of the gospels, who thus becomes the Jesus of experience and Jesus in history. The testimony of such men focusses on a certain point. When for instance Jefferson, the free-thinker, made his own Bible by putting together the ethical sayings of the gospels, when Lincoln said he would join the church that wrote over its doors the fatherhood of God and the brotherhood of man, when Gandhi—heir of another tradition—declares that he owes his passion for bringing separated human beings into fellowship to the Sermon on the Mount as well as to his Hindu scriptures, it is the ethical element in the religion of Jesus that evokes the response. This is more than his teaching. The power that he manifested in attacking the baffling issues of life is transmitted.

Additional evidence of where the vitality of the religion of Jesus originates can be seen in the response he gets from two opposite quarters—the poor and the well-to-do. There is an important fact behind the overworked claim that when the revolting proletariat rejects the church it also shouts for Jesus. This is more true in England than elsewhere and there it is true only in part. But what truth is in it means more than the fact that the oppressed find in him a champion of their rights, that his name historically stands for the release of those who are bound and sight to those who sit in darkness. It means that in him the universal righteousness and justice and good-will has got itself embodied in continuing fashion. When his name sounds, a bigger and more imperious fellowship than clan or creed or class flashes across our vision, a goal that can never be reached by any imperialism no matter how benevolent, by any dictatorship no matter how well meaning.

When this is understood many who to-day shout for him like those of old Jerusalem will, like them, go with him no further. This is manifestly true now with most of the prosperous. In the end most of our rich young rulers find his demands impossible. Does not our middle class democracy, which in its own glorification so freely uses his name as sanction, stand now in that position? In our educated comfort we middle class Americans think mostly of our obligation to serve by giving. Jesus em-phasized the obligation to serve by sharing. This calls democracy to fulfill itself in the distribution of economic power and the universalizing of cultural opportunity. But when it moves in this direction most of the well-to-do turn away from it and some of them invoke the sedition laws against those who make the proposals.

As for the rulers of plutocracy, like the lords of empire,

when they once sense the nature of the religion of Jesus, they usually proclaim him a menace—one who stirreth up the people. The bitter attack upon preachers for advocating reduction of armaments and outlawry of war, for opposing military training in high schools and colleges, for supporting international organization, identifies the vital element in the religion of Jesus. The same journals that attack the preachers who meddle with practical affairs commend as godly examples those who confine themselves to theological, exegetical, and liturgical exercises. A gospel that is merely simple, a worship that is beautiful but damned, can go on quite undisturbed by the principalities and powers of this world. But when theology raises ethical questions and beauty in worship stirs the wills of people to change their attitude toward their fellows and alter the behavior of the world then trouble begins also for them. The opposition that he receives outside and inside the churches, the response that he secures beyond the ranks of his professed followers, alike reveal the fact that the vital and challenging characteristic of the religion of Jesus is its ethical nature.

Here is a point at which the unlettered and the scholars agree. It is the Golden Rule and the Sermon on the Mount that express Jesus to the common people. Those who come to the gospel untrammeled by any of the doctrinal interpretations of ecclesiastical religion are inevitably impressed by their moral challenge. True the element of magic appears in the story, but the scholars tell us that the closer we get back to the actual words of the Galilean the clearer it is that his religion is essentially ethical, that this is the characteristic of the doubly attested sayings which are the most authentic part of the record. It appears that the work of corrupting the simplicity and softening the moral imperative of Jesus began early.

Taking the record as it now stands, with whatever has been added by its editors, one cannot read it and classify its religion as either theological, ceremonial, or institutional. It is still predominantly ethical. Jesus avoids discussing subtleties of doctrine with the Scribes; he puts human duties before the call to worship and makes its efficacy depend upon their fulfillment; he utterly condemns the mechanical devices of institutional religion. This central fact of the ethical nature of his religion is not sufficiently emphasized nor clarified by the recent books concerning it, probably because of the historic prejudice in Protestantism against the cultivation of morality. In failing to accept and proclaim this essential characteristic of his religion official Christianity is in the position that Jesus ascribed to the Scribes and Pharisees. It refuses to enter the Kingdom of Heaven itself and at the same time keeps out those who want to go in.

Yet the vitality of the religion of Jesus is sufficient to withstand this mistreatment. Despite continual corruptions and denials of his ethic by official Christianity it continually reasserts itself. It is dynamic not static. Has not every fresh realization of Jesus brought some new attack on the basic problems of community living, from the sharing of surplus wealth in the Jerusalem community and the higher sex standards of the Christians in the cities of the Roman empire, down through the social programs of the minority sects to the demands on the social order that follow the "Back to Jesus" movement initiated by modern biblical scholarship? Whence comes

[121]

the perennial protest against ecclesiastical corruption in organized Christianity? When the influence of Christian missions in the Orient is assessed what stands out more prominently than certain changes in moral attitudes and habits? How does it happen that the standards against which the younger men of the Orient are now measuring the behavior of the West are the same as those which her own inquiring spirits are using? Why is it that Western civilization is thus facing a judgment more searching than that which the philosophers brought to Rome in the day of her decline? Why is it that in the dawn of her imperialistic power the United States is being confronted with questions more penetrating than the eighth century prophets brought to Israel in the days of her new commercial prosperity ?

To say that the religion of Jesus is essentially ethical is not to say that he was merely an ethical teacher. It is conceded that he did not leave a theological system or a church organization or a social-economic program. Neither did he leave a set of ethical maxims. He left principles rather than precepts, teaching rather than teachings. Precepts are to be followed, principles are to be applied and developed. That is why his words are dynamic; they put creative obligation upon us. That is why men usually misinterpret and misrepresent Jesus when they expound his teachings separately. It is then that they are most apt to use him to support their own theology or politics or economics. Because the record is so fragmentary and so far removed from the figure it portrays, because also it consists of different interpretations of him, separate sayings and incidents have to be weighed according to the probability of authenticity, then grouped topically, to discover what central principles run through them.

Then it appears that Jesus is life as well as truth. To treat him merely as an ethical teacher, to put him in the same category as the Sophists or the Stoics is to miss the significance of his life and death, and to fail to receive the power of them. It matters not whether this is done by radicals or reactionaries—the result is the same—Jesus is lost. If men want only ethical teaching, they had better take Aristotle—he makes less trouble. But if they try Jesus, whose teaching is not apprehended until it becomes power for living, they will discover how to change the world and thereby how truly to enjoy it.

When this is not discovered by those who study and teach the gospels, it is because they are trying to appraise his message as teaching instead of testing it in life. It is also because we get our working philosophy of life and most of our religion elsewhere—from the Greeks and the Romans and our ancestral tribes. Hence our life is divided and we live in compartments. We have a theological or a liturgical religion, a philosophical morality, and a comfortable way of life, supported by a pecuniary organization of society and an imperial state. We uphold the institutions of our class, our nation, our race, and these often separate us from Jesus and his God because they divide us from the rest of mankind.

2. FROM THE BEGINNING

That the religion of Jesus is essentially ethical may be seen again by the merest glimpse at its origin and the course of its development. He himself never claimed to be the founder of a new religion. He proclaimed it to be his mission to fulfill the law and the prophets. He located himself as a point in an historic process. He personalized and universalized a racial movement, then committed it to his followers to continue.

It was not Judaism that Jesus developed, it was not the law of the Scribes and Pharisees that he was fulfilling, for they had made the commandment of God of no effect by their vain traditions. It was not any one of the Hebraic codes. It was that more vital law which ran in varying degree and vitality through all of them, constituting an exceptionally powerful attempt to order the ways of a people in righteousness and justice. This law was the embodiment of the prophetic message. It is the prophets of Israel who are the spiritual ancestors of Jesus. Without understanding and tracing that continuity he can neither be understood nor appreciated. To treat him as a separate voice coming suddenly from heaven, to view him as an isolated point in history—as the Christian tradition so generally does—is to fail to get his meaning and objective. To discuss his ethic without analyzing his relationship to the prophets is to deal in abstractions. Also, lacking historic perspective, this practice gives undue weight to the influence of the contemporary situation.

The prophets of Israel, particularly those of the eighth century, stand out as rarely creative men in the history of religion. Without understanding that, the ethical values in the religion of Jesus cannot be fully perceived nor developed. The religion of the Hebrew people began where all religion begins—in tribal life. In its earliest days it had the same characteristics as the faiths of the other Semitic tribes. Yet in the outcome it was utterly different. The same primary elements that became transformed by way of the Hebrews into the religion of Jesus whose end is not yet, developed also into the religions of Assyria and Babylon, which assimilated along with Judaism some of the ideas of Egypt and Persia and then passed with all those empires into the records of the dead. The remnants of early Semitic religion that survived among the desert folk were in due course transformed into Islam. What determined the difference in the course of these streams that rose in the same watershed? Why was it also as McCown has shown in *The Genesis of the Social Gospel* that ethical ideas and ideals which were in varying degree common to the whole Mediterranean world survived only in and through the Hebrew religion?

The answer lies first of all in two determining factors in the life of the Hebrew people—their slave revolt in Egypt and the eighth century prophets. What the Egypt experience did was to bind them in a covenant with a delivering God whose face was set against injustice and oppression and so to give their religion an abiding opposition to those evils. What the prophets did was to proclaim the ethical nature of the national deity and to get a glimpse of his universal validity. They interpreted God in terms of righteousness and compassion within and between the nations. They set a national religion on the road where later it was to meet the common experience and need of mankind.

It is altogether inadequate to portray the prophets merely as preachers of social righteousness. They laid the foundations of an ethical religion and the corner stone was an experience of God. It is a commonplace to say that the religion of Yahweh was an ethical monotheism.

That is just the kind of polysyllabic phrase in which the academic mind conceals reality even from itself. The challenging fact is that these Hebrew prophets experienced God as an ethical personality and proclaimed that such experience depended upon ethical living. Their knowledge of God was expressed in experimental not conceptual terms. They did not talk in the abstract phrases of the philosophers and theologians. To serve Yahweh was more than burnt offerings; it was to establish righteousness and justice in the land, it was to refrain from oppressing and cheating the poor as landowner or trader. To walk humbly with the Lord was to do justly and to show mercy to your fellow men. Thus they planted and cultivated in the soil of Israel the root of the Gospel message—that God is love and to have fellowship with Him men must have fellowship with one another.

The prophets did not merely say that God requires righteousness and justice, compassion and goodwill. For them these ethical qualities are His nature; they constitute His awe inspiring holiness. They are both an ideal to be sought and verifiable values of experience having authority and practical worth like the axioms of science. So their imperative is entirely different from that claimed by the absolutes of conceptual theology or philosophy; likewise their outcome. The latter lend themselves to the support of an authoritarian religion, an imperialist state, and a class organization of society. But to proclaim God as a dynamic ethical imperative, verifiable in human experience, makes for a democratic religion and a democratic society. With this kind of God common people may have fellowship. He is not concealed in mysteries and worshiped from afar. He does not have to be mediated by priests.

Naturally enough these men of Israel who experienced and proclaimed this kind of God caught a glimpse of his universality. Such as He could not be confined to any people. For the ethical values thus personalized are approved and sought after in some form by man wherever and whenever he has lived. Therefore they may paradoxically be described as absolutes of experience, no matter how relatively interpreted and developed in various times and places. As soon as God was seen—no matter how imperfectly—to be righteousness and justice, compassion and goodwill, it was certain that He was bound to become more than a tribal deity or the protector of a nation. It was equally certain that those who proclaimed this kind of God in Israel—like their successors elsewhere—should be declared traitors by all good patriots, led always by the priests of the king's house and of the property owners whose divine right succeeds that of the king.

As usually happens, the conflict between prophetic and conventional religion was made more acute in ancient Israel because the prophets' identification of the experience of God with ethical behavior came out of and took shape in, a bitter social conflict. What is called the Mishpat struggle had two aspects, as Wallis has graphically shown in his *Sociology of the Bible*. On the one hand it was a fight between Yahweh and the strange gods introduced by contact with the conquered inhabitants of Canaan, by commercial intercourse, and intermarriage with surrounding nations. On the other hand it was the class conflict that appears when a rising commercial group acquires financial superiority over peasant cultivators and begins to annex their lands through mortgage foreclosures. This development acquired unusual significance in Israel because of the relation of the landed patrimony of the families to tribal and national solidarity and so to the national religion. In destroying the ancient Mishpat, that is the rough justice of the old tribal folk ways, the rich men of the city were also destroying the bond between the nation and the God whom they believed had given them the land.

The prophets had a more ethical faith. In the attempt of the ancient Mishpat to secure justice and solidarity they saw Yahweh expressing himself. So its destruction was for them the destruction of a vital experience of God. This view also lies behind their denunciation of luxury, making it much more than the contempt of the country man for softer ways of living. The disintegration of community life by the rise of the cities was also to the prophets the attrition of the relation between the Hebrew people and their God. They stood for a religion of the people against a religion of empire which the upper classes were imitatively acquiring from surrounding cultures.

What the prophets did then was to see God in and through certain ethical values in the tribal folk ways, to experience him in the aspirations, ideals, and efforts that developed out of this connection. Thus God and social righteousness, God and economic justice were inseparably joined. The conflict between Yahweh and the foreign Gods was also a conflict between the greedy grabbing ways of the new city society and the sharing ways of tribal days and the serving ways of the countryside. In that struggle and behind it they found God, not beyond the stars. They taught no cosmogony. They had no speculative wisdom about the mysteries of life and death and the future beyond the grave. It is possible for religion when it centers on these things to forget the daily needs of men and so in the end to lose God. Nature deities and the cosmic being who is derived from them may be worshipped without regard to moral obligations. But not the God of the prophets. If unrighteousness goes unchecked, injustice unredressed, then "Though you make many prayers in my house I will not hear you, though you stretch forth your hands all the day long in my courts I will turn away mine eyes from you."

Where else in the literature of religion, until we come to the Gospels, do we find the differences in value between a ceremonial and an ethical religion set forth with such beauty and power as in the words of the Hebrew prophets? Where else, except in the words of Jesus, is the futility of unethical worship depicted with such finality? Because the religion of the Hebrews was and is always corporate in nature and expression, the ethical behavior which the prophets declared to be the condition of any contact with the eternal was always social. When some of them later gave the individual a new place in religion, he was still the individual viewed as a member of the community. It was in a religious community life that the God of the prophets was to be supremely expressed, there the divine justice and goodwill were to be realized. So the Deuteronomic code attempts to organize a community that would live in such social justice, compassion, and fellowship that God could dwell in its midst. But a rising commercialism committed this law, always more a vision than a reality, into the hands first of the priests with their ritual and then of the Scribes with their legalism. What these forces, allied with nationalism and commercialism, did with this attempt between the days of the prophets and Jesus is sufficiently well known by his scathing description of it to need no repetition or comment.

It is sometimes said by those who contemplate the ethical demands of Jesus that there is a perpetual conflict between him and civilization. Such conflict as there is he inherited from the eighth century prophets. But the phrase as it stands is misleading. Also it lends itself too easily to the mood of those who consider his ethic impossible and are loathe to face or undertake the changes that are necessary if Western society is to avoid the fate of its predecessors. It is not with civilization in the true sense of the word that the prophets and Jesus have a mortal quarrel, but with the evils that hitherto destroyed it. To set down this antagonism as merely one instance of the conflict between urban and rural society that occurs at a certain period in the story of every nation and is now troubling us is a misleading underestimate. True it came out of that situation, but it was the genius of the prophets to get a glimpse of the timeless aspect of local events, to perceive if but dimly that underneath was the struggle between the cohesive and destructive elements in life and the universe, and to declare on which side the Eternal Spirit might be found. Hence it is a misrepresentation of the prophets to put them down as mere critics of culture. Their critical function is important and superbly performed. But the worth of their positive appeal is no less. They call human life to develop its vital qualities and so to avoid decay. They point the way to the Beloved

Community. They show the ethical conditions of the Great Society. They add something essential to what the poets and philosophers have done in revealing the timeless in time, the abiding in the temporary, the ongoing in the transitory.

In the organized life of the Hebrews, then as now, the alien culture that is miscalled civilization won and the prophets lost. But at what a price! Certainly the city has some ethical qualities to contribute in its time to the developing life of man, has indeed the power to eliminate some of the unethical qualities of tribal days, to modify their barbarous cruelty and soften the war making attitude to outsiders. But the prophets declare that when the city destroys the cohesive virtues of the older, simpler community life it makes sure its doom. Let history say if they were right! What city state, what cosmopolitan empire, survived its failure to preserve the cementing capacity of the earlier stages of social organization? Rejecting the mutualism of simpler days in favor of the law of the jungle, giving to the strong what he could take and then passing it on by law to his heirs, they have all perished from the strife and luxury thus engendered. The tribes of the desert may be primitive but they live after the empires that their kinsmen built have fallen back into dust. Let those who now trust in the automatic capacities of city civilization, who regard its critics as mere reversions to an impossible past, find an exception to this course. Let those who can see no virtue in anything that belonged to yesterday, no value in any experience except modernity, ask themselves how much in his biological aspect man repeats the development of his ancestors. Then they can inquire whether the failure of civilization does not lie in its incapacity to develop the life giving portion of the experience of the past.

The experience of the Exile contributed to the forces that were obscuring and diverting the prophetic element in the Hebrew religion. What it did to stimulate repentance was in the end offset by what it did to fasten foreign ways upon the social and economic attitudes of the Jews and still more by what it did in depriving their religion of responsibility for the community life whose control now lay in alien hands. Under one influence religion pushed its social hope more and more into the future and in catastrophic terms, under the other it allied itself closer with the wealthy ruling class so that even its apocalyptic note became increasingly materialistic. To be dynamic religion must possess and transmit a great hope, must kindle its followers with the vision of a glorious future. This apocalyptic element becomes opiate or stimulus according to whether it appears in magical or ethical terms, according to the degree to which it calls for continuous human effort or is something to be suddenly done for man, who then has only to enjoy its splendor and its power.

The Messianic hope of the Hebrew prophets varied in this respect according to the political and economic situation, but in the main it was expressed in vigorously ethical terms. It usually depicted the reign of a great deliverer who was just and righteous altogether, who loved his people with an everlasting love and was an unfailing helper in their time of need. But by the time the Gospel story opens, as a result of the control of religion by and for the ruling class, this social hope had been transposed into material terms. As officially interpreted and commonly desired the reign of God was to be temporal prosperity and power for the Jews, the overthrow of the Roman and the setting up of the Jewish state, the extension of national power not the universal dominion of a God who was supreme above all other gods because he was the eternal spirit of righteousness, justice, and goodwill. Political revolution and abundance of earthly goods was what Jesus found expected of the Messiah. It was a combination that appears too often in the history of religions, but nowhere with less excuse than in that type of evangelical theology which promises to the saved the best—or is it the worst—of both worlds, prosperity here and heaven hereafter. This transposition of the prophetic hope joined with the diversion of the ethical requirements of the law into the formal obligations of petty ceremonials to produce a religion with no time or interest for the exactions which the rich were taking from the poor, or the corruption which was destroying them both.

The word of authority which Jesus threw into this situation, that fell with such strange and welcome power upon the ears of the people and was instantly rejected by the chief priests and rulers, announced the fulfillment of the law and the prophets. It was the prophets' declaration of the ethical nature of God and of the future that was possible for people who shaped their course in harmony with it that he developed. It was the law which sought after the righteousness of God in human relations that he fulfilled, not the law of the Scribes and the Rabbis whose fine ethical maxims were thoroughly fossilized by encrusting ceremonial minutiæ. Hence the point of the criticism that his loftiest sayings are to be found, at least in substance, in the Talmud is turned the other way.

When he uses them they sound otherwise and have a different meaning than in its pages. His quarrel with the official custodians and interpreters of the law is that they have lost the prophetic line, are no longer seeking after an ethical God to be known increasingly in human life. With the Pharisees who are seeking to revive the law he joins the issue because they not only fail to see it as a step in the search after the God of the prophets but they prevent that search by trying to make the law the basis for a conquering nationalism and so misrepresent and mutilate its God. By the same token he was out of sympathy with the more zealous nationalists who were planning immediate revolution against Rome. His revolutionary consciousness, which has recently been so much emphasized, was ethical and spiritual not political. He was concerned with the transformation of human nature, not the transfer of power. His way of release for Israel was through the development of the ethical religion of the prophets into a universal faith and striving, the redemption of the world in suffering and sacrifice.

It is the connection of Jesus with the prophets, and again particularly with those of the eighth century that determines the much debated question of whether his ethic was merely *ad interim*. The sayings of Jesus which the modern world finds so hard are those that relate to property and to force. He declares acquisitiveness to be the way to destruction not well-being, he substitutes goodwill for coercion as the basis of human relationships and organization. It is at these points that his ethic is declared impossible and explained away as being meant only for the brief period before the Kingdom of Heaven appeared and so unrelated to the needs of a continuing social order. But no one has yet shown anything like Jesus' sayings about wealth, nonresistance and the spiritual overcoming of evil in the apocalyptic literature current in his day. On the other hand, their roots can be seen plainly in certain similar words of the prophets. Instead then of being *ad interim* they have a long historic development and meaning. They represent attitudes essential to the continuity of human society. In so far as they have any relation to the apocalyptic element in the Gospels they signify that for Jesus that hope is cast in ethical terms, that he fulfills the ethical rather than the magical elements in the apocalyptic aspect of Hebrew prophecy.

It is thus the ancestry of the religion of Jesus that primarily determines its character. The fact that his spiritual lineage runs back to the prophets of the eighth century in Israel indelibly stamps his religion as predominantly ethical. One that fulfilled theirs could be nothing else. It is their overemphasis of the uniqueness of Jesus, added to the effects of their alliance with the powers of this world, that has prevented the churches formed in his name from understanding the ethical nature of his faith. His uniqueness lies in the quality and power of his contribution to the movement of which he proclaimed himself the fulfillment but not the end. He never claimed for himself that separateness from humanity or that absolute originality which the churches have too often claimed for him. On the contrary, he emphasized his representative character, his connection with an historic human movement. Herein he submits himself to the same test which he proclaims as the judgment for all similar claims and attempts—their value in experience, their contribution to the realization and improvement of life.

The wide response that he gets in all lands is further evidence of his representative character, though defenders of the faith often set it forth as testimony to his uniqueness. The struggle for an ethical religion is, of course, both older and wider than the line which runs back to the prophets of Israel. The attempt to develop the cohesive qualities of tribal and rural life in a city state is to be found in the religion of other races. But nowhere else has their vital challenge been as continuously developed as in this movement for which the Hebrew prophets were primarily responsible, which is embodied for the modern world in the personality of Jesus.

Those who now object to the use of his name in connection with current attempts at an ethical religion are to a large degree victims of the authoritarian manner in which the churches have been accustomed to use it. But there is an authority of experience to which all must submit or come to disaster. When chart and compass are verified, we either sail by them or we get lost or wrecked. So for those who acknowledge only the method of science the question of how much authority there is in Jesus is the question of how much he represents the experience of the past that demonstrably makes for the good life and how much he challenges men to continue the search for it. To use his name with any implication of finality is to deny his spirit. The genuine authority of any name in any section of human effort is determined by how much its owner contributed to that field and how much he inspires others to carry forward his efforts. To fail to accord due respect to such names is to lack historic sense. To fail to respond to their inspiration and challenge is to neglect a source of power.

3. THE FUNDAMENTALS

When the fragmentary nature of the Gospels that record the life of Jesus and the distance they are removed from him is frankly recognized, the current attempts to reconstruct his religion do not lack boldness. With such materials, what accuracy is possible except in outline? Of what can one be sure except central characteristics, general attitudes and trends? But if these are sufficiently consistent through the various interpretations and editings that make up the Gospel story, if they appear in the sources that are closest to the personality depicted, then it appears that we have its vital qualities.

The fact that there is no magic in the doubly attested sayings, conjoined with the fact that the ethical element in the Gospel story as it stands outweighs the magical incidents, even as it has later transcended all the magic and mystery which the churches have woven around the figure of Jesus, determines the main question. When it comes to characterizing his religion as either theological, ceremonial, or ethical, there can be no shadow of a doubt that the Gospel record as a whole confirms what scholars tell us about the nature of its most authentic sayings. The absence of anything like a theology in his teaching, his declaration that reality in worship depends upon meeting ethical obligation, that experience of the forgiveness and love of God is determined by the development of similar attitudes to our fellows, show clearly which aspect of religion Jesus considered primary. Only routine familiarity with his sayings can obscure the ethical nature of his demands upon his followers.

He wants not obeisance but life, not words but deeds.

His test is the fruits of the spirit. It is the failure to serve human need, not violation of ecclesiastical rules, that brings about separation from the eternal. For him, as for the scientist in the laboratory, the essence of faith is to dare and do—not to say words. Also that is the way to knowledge. It is he that doeth the will who finds the truth. The nature of this will saves all this from becoming another formal system, mere activism. For the will of God according to Jesus is not that men should observe the requirements of the law or pattern themselves after a code of ethics but that they should show certain attitudes toward each other which require the continual development of human conduct and relations, so that going the second mile becomes a general principle. Also the quality of life and of the religion behind it is revealed and tested by thought and motive, as well as by results in conduct. But the important place accorded to the latter saves Jesus' emphasis upon the inner life from becoming mere mysticism. It is only when conduct expresses and verifies desire that one experiences God by sharing his life.

(a) CONCERNING GOD

The first question to ask of any religion is what is the nature of its God. Upon this depends its valuation of man and the destiny it offers him. Strictly speaking, one should not speak of Jesus' view of God but rather of his relationship to God, for it is from this that we have to gather what his view was, since he makes no formal declaration of it. What is clear beyond dispute is that he trusted in a loving heavenly Father. The essence of his relationship with the eternal was the assumption that God was as lovingly concerned with men as a father with his children, always ready to forgive them, always eager to help them. To say that God is love is now too soft a phrase because of the sentimentality that has gathered around that word in the usage of the West, which enables many modern Christians to overlook the fact that the essence of the Kingdom of God according to Jesus is righteousness. This is the easier missed and the God of Jesus misrepresented in another direction because the essence of all human kingdoms is power. To speak of God as goodwill is nearer to the mind of Jesus. He constantly portrays the Eternal Spirit as willing good to all men, even to evildoers. This in a double sense is the will of God, for himself and for man. It is an active, sacrificing goodwill. It is willing to help men even to the point of suffering. Thus at last in the history of religion the element of sacrifice is made ethical.

It is thus the ethical God of the early prophets, not the cosmic God of the later Hebrew writers with whom Jesus had fellowship. It is almost impossible to find a word to represent the position of Jesus concerning the supreme being whom he calls heavenly Father. It is more unconsciously held than a declared conviction. It is of greater reach and depth than an hypothesis, though it serves as a working basis for life. He simply assumes the existence and nature of God as one assumes that the sun will rise to-morrow. That assumption is a part of his being, a condition of his life like the air he breathes. Perhaps the word presupposition comes as near as any to expressing the part that the ethical nature of God plays in his thinking and life, though that is inadequate.

In one or two sayings Jesus does refer to the God of the cosmos and about him he makes the same assumption as about the Great Companion and Redeemer of man.

His sun and rain are bestowed alike upon the evil and the good, the just and the unjust; he watches with concern the destiny of the least of his creatures. This trust in a personal goodwill in and behind the universe may seem utterly naïve to the modern mind and may be quite impossible for this sophisticated generation, but how does it look from the standpoint of results in human life when compared with other gods. Since the millions even under a godless communism, and indeed most of the intellectuals, insist on having some sort of a god, what kind they get is of some importance even to the few who find one unnecessary or impossible. At least to ascribe justice, compassion, and goodwill to the spirit of the universe does not make life more greedy and brutal, more callous and selfish. At least the God of Jesus is ethical above all other gods, and with that fact those who think that the destruction of the cosmogony of traditional Judaism and Christianity by the newer astronomy and physics has ended the value of the Gospel record for modern men have yet to reckon.

Judging by his recorded attitude to those who differed from him, Jesus would be the last to expect that men to-day would interpret the nature of the universe in precisely the same form he did. The essential thing is the assumption that there is support in the cosmos for the moral aspirations of man, help for him in his ethical struggle. This is something which is capable of demonstration only by experiment. Since in the absence of proof some assumption has to be made, the question is which assumption—hostility, indifference, or friendliness—leads to the better results in human living. Also which leaves man in the better position if the facts finally disprove it.

Here again this generation seems inclined too much to an either-or dilemma. The facts do show that the cosmos is partly hostile to man at certain points and indifferent at others. But there is still room for the assumption that it is friendly to him at vital points. Not to make the necessary effort to find out whether this assumption will hold is to miss the only chance to overcome the hostility and endure the indifference. This is one value then in the religion of Jesus for the modern man. He suggests how to avoid the futility and nihilism of The Modern Temper, and he puts the cosmic problem in its place.

It is not merely in the fact that his God is ethical that the value of the religion of Jesus for the modern world appears. It develops more particularly in the way this God is experienced and known. Relationship with him is established and verified by relationships with men. He requires not duties but the attitudes from which duties follow. To gain his forgiveness one must forgive one's fellows. It is an equal and identical obligation to love him with all heart and mind and spirit and to love one's neighbor as one's self—the neighbor being the one in need no matter how separated by class distinction, racial prejudice, or religious animosity. Failing this the love of God is nothing more than a pious illusion, a temporary warming of the heart that soon leaves ashes in its place. So the apostle who understood the essence of the God whom Jesus talked about and lived with asks how a man can love the God he has not seen if he does not love the brother he sees constantly. This is not easily done by those who live in a civilization based on power, for that is the opposite of love. Especially is it difficult for those of the privileged class who share in the power or derive benefits from it. They may perceive that love is the greatest thing in the world—the source and mainstay, the redemption and immortal hope of life; but to live as though it were is another matter. Yet this is the only way the word becomes reality—it has to become flesh or it dies.

So it was that the great apostle to the Gentiles, so often charged with giving Christianity a different direction from that in which Jesus set out, declares that without the continuous development of love, all else in the name and behalf of religion—eloquence, insight, knowledge, benevolence, martyrdom—is unavailing. Again it appears that in this God who is goodwill there is all power but there is no softness. Paul was but reiterating the teaching of Jesus—as he repeated that of the prophets—that no formal virtues, no subtlety of creeds, no multiplying of gifts, can atone for the failure to serve and share with those in need. "Inasmuch as ye did it not unto the least of these my brethren ye did it not to me" is the final word because it recognizes that separation from the eternal spirit of goodwill is an accomplished fact, brought about by the manner of life.

Here is something different from the flabby glad hand of a merely sentimental evangelicalism that has been able without knowing how or why it was done, to breed and train and then decorate with honorary degrees, and even anoint with congratulatory tears when they escape the penitentiary, some of the corrupters of our public life in this generation. The fellowship—it is a truer word to-day than either kingdom or reign—which Jesus bade men seek and invited them to enter is a fellowship with each other and with God, increasing in both directions, and it involves something more than love or goodwill. That was the element which Jesus developed so much further than the prophets. But it was the righteousness of God which he bade men seek, insisting that the realization of the fellowship depends upon the finding of the righteousness. The word justice does not seem to have been used by Jesus but that its content is implied follows from his connection with the prophets. He is developing their assertion that realization of God depends upon the increase of righteousness and justice between classes, nations, races, as well as individuals. Confined to the latter the search for justice becomes itself recorded in mere formulæ that are increasingly twisted to the sanctifying of injustice.

The love of God for man, the love of man for God, and the love of man for man—which are so interdependent and intertwined in the word and life of Jesus—are not understood and apprehended unless it is remembered that they root in the soil of justice and can only grow as that soil is kept rich and vital. In no religion does the ethic depend so absolutely and constantly upon the nature of its God as in the religion of Jesus. In other religions the ethic can become better than the gods, but not here. Here a far flung ideal calls and challenges. Men are urged to strive to be like this ethical God. They are condemned not by a code but only for failure to struggle in this direction. Hence the inexorable nature of the love expressed in the Gospels. In the judgment parable we have no arbitrary whim of an absolute authority, but a revelation of the inevitability of spiritual law. It was not failure that was damning, for there is always forgiveness. It was the absence of effort to help others that brought about separation from God. This sternness appears on occasion concerning the ordinary bread and butter relations of life. Righteousness like love, is not left in the realm of the abstract or in the atmosphere of sentiment. As with the prophets, Jesus makes it concrete in day by day economic affairs. Exactions in mortgages on widows' houses and monopoly profits on temple offerings make the profession of religion vain. Salvation comes, even to that pariah the taxgatherer for Rome, when unjust gains are restored.

Thus there is nothing stultifying to man in the God of Jesus as there is in the God of many of the Christian theologies. He is not absolute in the sense that they are. He does not inhibit human development and stop human inquiry by demanding obedience to some final commands or submission to some finished revelation. He is not that aspect of the universe before which man is helpless, which overwhelms him by its refusal to yield to his inquiry, or its indifference to his moral aspirations. That quality of the cosmos and its bearing upon human effort has been overemphasized in certain of our theologies and in the thinking of our younger intellectuals. In both cases the result is paralysis of the moral will.

The reason that the unyielding aspect of the universe is practically unrecognized by Jesus is that for him the knowledge of God comes by ethical insight and experience rather than by the intellectual process. Whether or not this is a deficiency depends upon what attitude his religion enables man to take to that aspect of the cosmos when he faces it; also upon its capacity to coördinate with the approach to God through reason. The essential thing about the God of Jesus is that he requires creative effort from man. He not only does not inhibit the constant revaluation and reconstruction of life, he positively demands it. To do his will is to seek righteousness, pursue truth, develop goodwill. He is on the side of change not inertia. If it should appear to the modern mind that God himself is not finished, but is the eternal striving, that view would not be uncongenial to the attitude of Jesus.

It should always be remembered that Jesus urged man to an experience of God similar to his. But that was and is too high a religion for most of his followers. Soon they began to put him between men and God, then to make him into God or an aspect of God. The test of what they have thus done with him is whether they have diminished or increased the creative ethical urge and power which is the vital element in his relation to the eternal. Is the search for higher forms of living stronger in the religion about Jesus than in his? This is a twofold test, determining on the one hand the fidelity of organized Christianity to him, on the other its value for modern life. It is because Jesus' experience of God is ethically creative that his kind of God cannot be used to support an autocratic, imperialistic, class privileged form of human organization. Fellowship with that kind of God requires the continuous democratization of life, beginning with the institutions of religion. The Reformation started Protestantism in this direction, with the universal priesthood of all believers as its distinctive emphasis. But gradually the absolute book replaced the absolute church in preventing men from developing their vital experience of God in human relationships. Then the distinctive doctrine of justification by faith was so misinterpreted as to give men assurance of salvation while ignoring their complicity in those sins of the corporate life which according to the prophets and Jesus inexorably alienate God from men. Then inevitably those who guard and teach the doctrine and the book assumed again the functions, prerogatives, and powers of priests. Thus Protestantism in some quarters is losing its essential genius and attempting once more to mediate God to men—this time through experts—instead of helping them to experience God for themselves in all human relationships as the religion of Jesus requires.

The completion of the Reformation, the fulfillment of its attempt to realize the ethical God of Jesus in place of the absolute God of Rome, requires the acceptance of the universal function of prophecy by all believers. This means that they all seek the development of the experience of God in terms of human relationships through constant efforts to revalue and reconstitute them on the basis of justice and goodwill. Thus there comes together in that working fellowship which Jesus urged men to seek the humanity of God and the divinity of man. The outworking result is the spiritualizing of life not the secularizing of religion, of which there has certainly been plenty. Then God is worshiped in spirit and in truth, he is glorified by the increasing incarnation of his righteousness and goodwill, not by giving him the adoration and tribute that an absolute monarch demands and upon which he fattens always at the expense of the subjects. In a democratic world the idea that God can be satisfied by any kind of tribute can survive only as absolute monarchy still survives in word and emotional reaction after it has become archaic as a form of government. According to Jesus fellowship with God is sought not because God requires it but because it is the highest and most satisfying experience, it becomes life eternal. To know and seek God in and through the fellowship of men in serving, sacrificing, goodwill, in the establishment of justice in all the relations of life, gives us a living, growing religion, develops at one and the same time the potentialities of man and the inexhaustible riches of His grace. We have no finished revelation, no completed wisdom, no perfect pattern of life, but the ongoing search, the endless striving, the continuing attainment.

(b) ABOUT MAN

In determining the quality and worth of a religion its estimate of man is as important as its representation of God, and these two are interdependent. It is customary to say that a distinguishing characteristic of Jesus is the supreme value that he gave to personality, and thereafter to declare that respect for persons is the essential ethical quality of the Christian religion, the great contribution it has to make to life. This statement rests not upon any formal declaration of Jesus but upon the fact that underneath his utterances concerning his fellow human beings and his attitudes toward them there lie certain assumptions or presuppositions concerning human nature similar to those he held concerning the nature of God. In his appeals to them, especially to those whom society usually condemns as hopeless, he assumes that human nature is capable of unlimited moral development. His faith in the recuperative capacity of man's moral nature is similar to that of modern medical science concerning his physical being, and similarly justified. As Nash used to say, a belief in "the infinite worth of the down-most man" is one of his basic working principles. This not only anticipates the modern view of the improvability of human nature that underlies our social programs, it goes deeper. With Jesus this was no platform phrase, no professional formula. He was willing to die for it.

Many of our younger writers have revolted against the tragic era in literature and life. Its fallacy they declare was that it thought too highly of human nature. But there is such a thing as thinking too meanly of man. The realism that sees only man's present estate, and therefore has ground for regarding his failures and incapacities as outweighing his achievments, is really not realism at all but only romanticism looking in another direction. The record shows that Jesus had no illusions about his fellows. Was not Judas in his inner circle? He had cause enough to know the fickleness and brutality at the bottom, the corruption and cruelty at the top of organized society. Yet he continued to believe in the moral reserves of humanity.

This is not only because he assumes the unfailing goodness of God—his capacity to forgive and to help man—limited only by man's unwillingness to be forgiven and helped. It is also and likewise because he assumes the capacity of man to respond to an ethical God. For him man's moral development appears to be a process of action and reaction between man and God in both directions. With Jesus, confidence in man's improvability is confidence in his capacity for fellowship with the ethical God whom he called Heavenly Father, and likewise with his fellow human beings, in ever enlarging justice and goodwill. Again it needs to be insisted among Western individualists that Jesus does not view human nature as

separate beings. It is in their capacity for mutual development that he believes—both among themselves and
between themselves and the eternal. It is in this twofold
relationship that we get beyond the accepted meaning of
the term moral. It is the spiritual capacity and development of man that therein appears. But the process is
concretely ethical.

(c) REGARDING SALVATION

It follows from Jesus' assumptions concerning the
nature of man and of God that the salvation made available by his religion consists in ethical development
coöperatively pursued and realized. In its beginning
organized Christianity derived its power from its offer of
salvation to man. To-day the word has fallen into deserved
disrepute because of the selfish escape from the battle of
life and the immoral exemption from its pains and penalties which the churches have too generally offered in the
name of Jesus. But as the evidence for the decay of Western civilization makes its way into the consciousness of
modern man he will begin to talk more about saving it,
and himself with it. Then it will be well for him to know
that the way of salvation which the religion of Jesus opens
is in a different direction from that usually offered in
traditional Christianity, and at the very points where he
finds that to be unethical and stultifying.

Indeed in the religion of Jesus salvation is not offered
at all. It is not a gift, but a search. It is not something
done by church or book or God for man, but something
achieved by God and man together. It is not a plan into
which man fits like an automaton but a process in which
he coöperates. It is no imitation of a perfect being. It
is not purchasable from any church confident of holding

the keys of heaven and hell, or claiming the only formula for divine forgiveness and fellowship—either by faithful obedience to ecclesiastical commands, profession of sound doctrine, great gifts, or good works. It develops the creative not the possessive faculties. So it is not magical by professing to do something for man which he can and ought to do for himself. Because it is mutual, it neither views him as a poor worm helpless in the dust nor urges him pridefully to attempt the impossible. Instead of stultifying him with a final revelation it requires his continual development. It is progressively realized.

Historically the salvation Christianity proclaims for man is forgiveness from his sins and assurance of fellowship with God. At its best this has involved repentance and restitution, required the abandonment of evil and the going on to perfection, the continuous development of the graces of the spirit. At its worst it has provided a magical and emotional sanction for immorality, public and private. But this is a gross perversion of the religion of Jesus. When the apostles told people to believe on Jesus and they should be saved, the evidence concerning the way the early Christians lived shows that what was meant was that they should have power to free themselves from the corruptions of the Roman world. With the apostles salvation was not, any more than it was with Jesus, a magical exemption from the arbitrary commands of an offended deity; it was a way of overcoming concrete evils in human life.

There is a current mood which denies sin as it does God, declaring one as outworn as the other, asserting that there remains only immorality and crime. Yet there is still both the fact and the problem of evil. There is still man

[150]

the destroyer as well as man the creator, doing violence to himself and his fellows, mutilating both his works and his nature. All religions offer man some solution to the problem of evil, and some deliverance from its power. This is either by escape or conquest. The religion of Jesus requires the active overcoming of evil. It gives men no refuge from the struggle of life. It calls for continuous change of persons and society. It brings not the peace of passivity, of a quietism that has abandoned the fight against the world, but a peace arising in the midst of the conflict out of a realization of its meaning and a sense of being allied with the eternal.

This religion also has in it something of the turbulence that troubles nature at times. Instead of asking men to passively receive the benefits of the passion of God it asks them to share in it. Those forms of Christianity which center on emotional satisfactions are perversions of the religion of Jesus. He called men to take up a cross like his, not to look possessively to his cross for redemption. Therefore his religion is dynamic. It sets men at work at the biggest of all tasks—the overcoming of evil—and for power it connects them with the eternal energy.

At this point is the essential contrast with the religion of Buddha which also proclaims the progressive conquest of evil. But its achievement is the overcoming of desire in and by the individual. It is pure escape from the evil of the world, which is left in its hopeless condition. Also in Nirvana there is a fixed point to be attained—the final conquest of desire, the absorption in the all. When modernized Buddhism stands for the highest ethical development of personality, when it adopts social service and reform, it is in spite of not because of the original teaching. This will be even more true if it ever makes a revolutionary attack upon an unethical order. But with Jesus there is an ideal to be continuously realized and, because it is the unfolding of certain capacities of human nature which Jesus holds also to be the essential qualities of God, there is no point at which man can be satisfied.

Here again is the vital contact with the religion of Confucius which also is ethical. But its salvation consists in the ability to live within a series of human relationships in a fixed pattern. These are designed to give peace and contentment; also to keep society stable with the support of the Lord of Heaven, who is an enlarged nature deity just as the god of the Hebrew prophets is an enlarged tribal patriarch. But the result is morally leagues apart. China has had a static religion supporting a static society. Those who received the religion of the prophets and of Jesus have had among them a rebellious urge toward righteousness and goodwill in society and in persons. This difference is partly due to the fact that one religion was the ripe fruit of a stratified society while the other was a revolt against such stratification at its first appearance. Those who think that a purely pragmatic ethic, developed in a society which accepts and sanctifies by law the division of the classes, can find the way into the future will do well to observe and ponder several thousand years of history in China.

There is a similar contrast to be made between the continuous demand of the religion of Jesus for repentance and purification of life and much of the theology that has been promulgated in his name. Because he calls men to overcome evil by replacing it with other attitudes and deeds, and to the pursuit of a far-flung ideal of righteousness and fellowship, the offer in his name of a finished plan of salvation which represses both man's intellect and moral striving is a complete denial of his religion. Its supreme ethical quality is its challenge to man to continuously develop his nature, his society and his experience of God. In this respect it is much more congenial to the spirit of science than to that of some theologies.

Our liberal Protestantism has so far failed to appreciate the developmental character of the religion of Jesus. Its exponents are apt to speak of the application of his principles to modern life as though they were some final formula, the last word about civilization. But his characteristic injunctions were seek, learn, do. He was free from that fatal fault of the founders of religions when they leave a finished system for their followers to proclaim. This has always been one of the root causes of the later corruptions of once pure faiths. They had no room for development. They evoked no moral energy. If we are to be true to Jesus when we speak of the application of his principles we must mean their development. The only way in which they can be applied and remain ethical is when they are treated as working principles to be carried further by the process of experimentation. Here again Jesus is nearer to the procedure of science than to that of traditional theology. When the Sermon on the Mount is put in its place in the perspective of social evolution it ceases to be an absolute morality, ceases also to be an impracticable counsel of perfection, becomes instead a concrete challenge to realize the possibilities of human living.

When religion unwittingly betrays man by offering him an escape from evil that in the end only leads him into deeper bondage to the world, it is because it thinks of sin and salvation only in terms of the individual. The salvation that opens in the religion of Jesus is corporate. This is to say more than that it is for the associated life as well as for the individual. Because it is a twofold mutual process between man and man and between man and God, because it can be realized progressively only in both these associations, it is corporate in its nature.

It is often said that Jesus discovered the individual, because of his emphasis upon the supreme value of personality. True enough he addressed himself mostly to individuals, but not to the individual viewed separately from society. That person is a fiction of the Western world. If Jesus heard the word used in this sense he would not know what we were talking about. He was a Jew and the Jew has preserved the tribal consciousness. If he ever exists apart from his racial community he has ceased to be a Jew. Jesus was the heir of the prophets and for them religion is the relationship between God and the people of Israel, between God and persons always as members of the nation. It was therefore just as natural for Jesus as it is difficult for men who are the heirs of the Western tradition of individualism, intensified by pioneer life and the Protestant religion, to apprehend the social nature of the self. With him that also was a presupposition. His good news of the Kingdom of Heaven presupposes what modern sociology formally declares, that the individual is fulfilled only as a member of an increasingly organic community, that society is meaningless unless it is justified and realized in the lives of all its members.

There is for Jesus no such division between the social and the personal gospel as we Western individualists, with our crude and partial psychology now make. For him they are interdependent aspects of religion just as man and society are interdependent aspects of human life. It would be impossible for Jesus to fall into the fallacy of regarding society as made up of separate persons that still plays havoc with our religion. Only recently two of our prominent religious writers have spoken of the relation of personal salvation to the redemption of society as though it were a process of addition, though they would disavow the position that religious effort must be concentrated on personal evangelism in order that society may ultimately be saved. The actual interacting process between the person and the group is reflected in the two aspects of the Kingdom of Heaven presented by Jesus; he urges men both to receive it and to enter into it. What happens whenever ethical development is realized is that some individuals get ahead of society and society then gets ahead of some of its sections. When this occurs some advance for the whole follows.

The corporate nature of the religious life that Jesus urged men to seek is seen again in his attitude toward evil in the concrete. Usually the attitude of official religion toward sin is negative. It offers indulgences or ecclesiastical pardon or the personal assurance of divine forgiveness. At its best it seeks to get men to turn away from sin, which is the violation of divine decrees, the ordinances of the church, or the conventional moral standards. With Jesus sin is more than this. What Jesus condemns particularly is what prevents men from entering into the fellowship that he regards as the supreme good. For him life is not bounded by decrees, divine or human. It moves ever toward a high goal—that Beloved Community in which the creatures of time and the timeless spirit find themselves realized together. It is then this goal that determines what is evil. For him the mortal sins are the acts and attitudes that make fellowship impossible, that separate man from man and therefore man from God. So the process of working out salvation is a process of getting rid of the separating facts, tempers and policies. This is a vital aspect of the ethical problem. Otherwise life cannot become mutual and organic.

What makes behavior sinful for Jesus can be seen in the difference between his attitude toward the outcasts of society and toward the pillars, also in those sayings about the rich and their possessions which are such a stumblingblock to those who live in the acquisitive society. It is hard for the rich man to enter into the Kingdom because his capacity and possessions limit the possibility and need of its fellowship. Riches choke the seed of the Kingdom because their pursuit and care require the cultivation of other qualities than fellowship, not because they prevent the spiritual life viewed as mystic withdrawal from economic necessity. It is similar with his relation to economic justice. He is not interested in dividing possessions. He has no time for that. What is the use if they are counted the supreme good. But to proclaim in his name a religion that makes men content to either suffer or benefit by injustice is as false to him as to say that to discuss the meaning of his principles in terms of economic justice is to degrade him into a minister to the stomach. It is Jesus' plain teaching that the struggle for economic necessities regardless of justice and fellowship is both futile and destructive. Do the facts of modern life contradict or confirm him? It is his declaration that the economic necessities are to be provided only by seeking for

[156]

justice and fellowship. Then their provision becomes uniting instead of separating, evil not good, spiritual not material. If men could realize that economic goods and services are to be adequately secured only by the cultivation of ethical values, will they not be more likely to use them for that purpose and so to avoid the enervating and corrupting consequences of what we now call prosperity.

It is concerning this matter that Protestantism, particularly in the wealthiest country in the world, needs to search its own soul. In so far as it has cultivated and strengthened the economic virtues, it has helped to develop the separating qualities of life—to produce the divisions of modern society, and the cleavage now appearing between this country and the rest of the world with the consequent renaissance of reliance upon force. Thus unwittingly it has nullified what it has done in urging men to seek the Beloved Community, just as through its participation in the production of concentrated property it has helped to destroy those graces of the spirit it has been seeking to cultivate. This looks like the corporate aspect of that old conflict between the flesh and the spirit with which Paul wrestled. If the higher values of society cannot win the victory over its appetites it must perish as does the body from overindulgence in the lusts of the flesh. If organized religion is ever to save the world it will have to renounce its sinful allegiance to the acquisitive society and develop the teaching of Jesus concerning the subordination of the practical aspects of economic behavior to its ethical possibilities.

It is at this point that the nature of the destiny urged on man by the religion of Jesus connects his religion with the cosmic problem. Among the occasions that separate man from fellowship with his fellow human beings and so from God there is none more potent than the manner in which he handles the physical resources of the universe. It is when he uses them for his own sustenance or cultural development before or against that of others that there arise divisions and conflicts. Here is the taproot of war. Thus the field of ethics covers the relations of man to the cosmos as well as his relation to his fellows. One of its basic problems then is the behavior of man, jointly and severally, toward the physical resources upon which all alike depend for nourishment and development. Thus ethically as well as physically man is involved with nature. He is not separated from it just because he can stand off and look at it, any more than he is separate from himself because he can stand outside himself. The antithesis between the natural man and civilization that leads Krutch in *The Modern Temper* into utter nihilism disappears when man sets himself resolutely to the ethical use of nature for mutual development. The supposedly civilized man is dehumanized only because he is unethical and therefore uncivilized.

Also those who use the resources of nature ethically—that is mutually—do not find the cosmos so indifferent as do Krutch and those for whom he speaks. They too—like the unethical religionists they abhor—are the victims of our fallacious Western individualism. Their view of the cosmos also is too egocentric. Nature is not so careless of life in the mass as it is of the individual. There is both origin and development of species. Races die out but man remains—at least for more than a million years. Like other species he remains and develops according as he learns to practice mutual aid. The cosmos proves to some degree favorable to those who use it coöperatively instead of destructively.

So much connection then is observable between the energy of the physical universe and that which is expressed in the moral struggle of man. Our capacity to discover more about the relation between these two forms of energy obviously depends upon the use we make of what we know, just as does our capacity to understand and use the physical aspect of the universe for sustenance and culture. Only as we experimentally develop mutual aid can we discover how much the universe lends itself to the support of that effort. The cosmic problem does not yield itself to the physical sciences alone. Its solution involves the nature and use of moral as well as physical energy. This is another reason why the ethical problem is the first business of religion. We know enough about the response of the cosmos to those who live in mutual aid to justify us in proceeding further in that direction. It is our only hope for truth as it is our only chance for life. The modern temper has arrived at the dead end of nihilism because it declares the hypothesis necessary for experimentation in life and discovery of truth to be itself impossible. But those who are temperamentally unable to take the necessary attitude of trust in the universe and in their fellows at least owe this much to the scientific spirit they profess to serve, that they should encourage and not attack the explorers.

Thus the ethical salvation that Jesus urges men to seek brings us in sight of a larger goal than the saving of civilization. It appears that whatever chance the race has of avoiding extinction, either by its mad and greedy waste of the known resources of the universe in competitive struggle or by failure to discover and use new means of life as these become exhausted, lies in mutual endeavor and the mutual administration of its capacities. Here the fact that the way of life that Jesus urges gives us not a pattern but a process of life takes on a wider reach and meaning. It is a process that runs beyond as well as through history. Behind his word lies first of all a part of the ancestral experience of the race. His ethic runs back to the tribal society in which all civilization had its origins. It continues and develops that mutualism and solidarity of tribal days which were gradually lost as city states with their class divisions succeeded village communities only to coalesce into great empires maintained by force. These have gone down in destruction because for the power and the glory they forsook the life giving qualities of sharing and serving. These values have been preserved in humble groups many of whom have been wiped out in blood and most of them neglected by the historians who have told the might of the empires and the majesty of the churches that crushed them.

The Hebrew people have the clearest record of a persistent attempt to develop tribal morality into a social ethic in the name and power of religion. It runs back from their great prophets in city days, through the judges of village times and the slave revolt in Egypt, to their nomadic life. The moral conflict created by prophetic religion still divides the Jewish people, even as that developed by the ensuing religion of Jesus usually sets the leaders of the Christian churches against those who take up his way of life to turn it into a highway for the nations.

Those who cannot find any continuity of ethical development, those apostles of modernity who think history must begin anew with us, and those who reject the ethic of Jesus because they hold the standards of simpler days to be unavailable for a complex society, might consider the process by which nervous organisms, species, and a social order came from simple cells. It now appears that mutual aid is not only the power of cohesion and continuance for human society but is also, biologically speaking, the vital aspect of the race. It is the secret of man's emergence as a species and the hope for his continuance. It is thus the deathless part of man's racial inheritance which is embodied in Jesus, which he declares to be the life of God seeking to express itself in men. It is then the way of life in the farthest sense to which Jesus invites.

Thus there is a deeper reason for the universal response to his ethic than its relation to the early experience of all nations. In it there sounds the call of that urge to live which runs back through all their ancestors in all the animate world, which is as social as it is personal. It is because this urge inextricably blends self-preservation and self-sacrifice, because it leads individuals to find themselves by living and dying for the species, and then for society and its institutions, that the continuity of life becomes possible. It is because the capacity to share, to serve and to suffer that others may live survives amid all the instinctive brutality and organized selfishness of modern life, because it becomes increasingly a mutual dedication to a chosen social order, that there is hope for the future. Here is a way of life that resists dissolution and defies the grave. For the pomp and circumstance, the power and the glory, over which men fight there is no continuance; only the inevitable dust and ashes. But for the spirit of mutual aid, the striving and the seeking for a way of life for all, there is no death.

It is then in the destiny to which it calls men and the response which that evokes, much more than in an intellectual perception of the nature of its origins or its God, that the ethical value of the religion of Jesus appears. It establishes a relation between the things of time and those which are timeless that calls man to continuous creative activity. Ethics has to do with the things of time. Religion proclaims itself a revelation of the timeless. An ethical religion relates these two, so that man who has to live in both worlds may find the meaning of life in making one serve the other, may discover wholeness by perceiving an infinite development in their coördination.

4. IN WHICH DIRECTION

The main point, however, in determining the ethical values in the religion of Jesus is not the impetus it gives the Western mind—long enough engaged in establishing essential differences—to discover the organic relations between the various aspects of life. Its chief value to modern man lies in the direction in which its projection into the unmapped territory of the future would move our organized life. Again it must be said with all possible emphasis that this is not a question of programs. These develop according to time and place and their demand for choice and judgment provides the means for ethical development.

Because the religion of Jesus is the expression of a process, it points only a general direction for the organized life of humanity. Because this process is visible in some degree everywhere in the record of the race, because it runs back into the whole course of life before man appeared upon the planet, the religion of Jesus transcends time and place, and offers something for universal development. Such authority as it possesses then as a guide to the general course of life derives not from any words of Jesus nor any doctrines about him, but is rooted in his representative character. From this point of view the argument about his sinlessness, on both sides, is irrelevant. His worth is determined by what experience shows and may show is the need of man to follow that trend in his life story—beginning with the origin of species—which Jesus represents.

There is no doubt about the general direction in which this trend would carry our organized life. It moves ever toward the solidarity of the human race. Jesus trusts in the capacity of man, aided by the eternal spirit, to develop his need and desire for fellowship until it overcomes his tendency toward conflict and removes the resultant subordination of the weaker to the will and ends of the stronger. So do all who believe in social evolution. If there is such a thing at all it means that the trend toward solidarity becomes stronger than the trend toward conflict and separation. Manifestly the possibility of a world community appears and grows only as the tendency toward solidarity is consciously chosen and developed, as the ties of kinship develop into a common search for the ideal. This is precisely what the religion of Jesus does and requires. To the common people everywhere he stands for the brotherhood of man. What that is and may be is for those who come after him to discover.

The movement toward solidarity is also the movement toward equality, the two being interdependent. Equality in the opportunity for development and in the exercise of power is the goal of political and economic evolution. It was sought and professed by democracy only to be abandoned when the concentration of wealth divided the people. Equality in access to such nourishment as exists and such culture as is available is characteristic of tribal society before slavery appears, being guaranteed by its solidarity—of which indeed it is the condition. It is unnatural, and considered either impossible or undesirable, in a wealthy, stratified society, except for pious talk about equality of opportunity after the capacity and desire to use opportunity has been made unequal by hereditary and environmental influences. Yet it remains as an aspiration and has been expounded as an American philosophy. And if there is to be that world community which the machine needs to fulfill its capacities to aid the development of man there must be a constant approach to equality between persons, nations, and races. It is in this direction that the development of the religion of Jesus would take mankind. Even those who deny any social content or meaning to his teaching proclaim with pride its guarantee of spiritual equality for all human beings. But if there is behind this principle no social process nevertheless it impels toward one, it cannot be proclaimed without developing its corollary in practical affairs.

When it comes to the more specific bearing of the teaching of the Gospels upon the course of human life the principles of Jesus are usually set forth in terms of personality, service, and brotherhood. Responding to the influence of our traditional individualism and its fatuous emphasis upon individual initiative, we are more apt to stress the need to develop the value of all persons than we are to stress the nature of the brotherhood in which alone persons become possible, or the character of the service in which alone personality is fully realized—especially its sacrificial element. Also it is quite possible to talk about these principles in terms of abstract ethical qualities without developing any urge or imperative for changing the present course of life, or arousing any opposition.

This cannot be done however with those principles of Jesus which more directly and concretely affect the organization of society. It is true that Jesus emphasized these in personal attitudes, but if we take them as working principles for the organization of society we find them to be basically different from those around which society is now carrying on its affairs. One is that all relations between human beings should be based on goodwill not power. The other is that life is realized only as the pursuit and enjoyment of material possessions and satisfactions are made subordinate to the development of ethical capacities. The principles that govern industrial society are opposite to these. However much it may desire goodwill and seek the things of the spirit, like all preceding civilizations its controlling principles are the right and duty of the strong to rule and the desirability of material possessions and satisfactions. It is imperialistic and acquisitive; power and greed are its dominating forces. It has even come to trust them for its future. Its imperialism is to be both benevolent and efficient because the successful in the money-making conflict have thereby proved themselves the most able and are now to be the most humane. By way of money the acquisitive society expects to find all good. Its citizens will not go hungry for an ideal. They will be well fed and will be allowed to pursue only as much of the ideal as the successful money-makers think is good for them.

It is now a commonplace that the way of Jesus takes the world away from war. His principle is usually stated as the replacing of force by love, but it is broader than that. It is the substitution of goodwill for power, and the place of force in organized society derives therefrom. This Gandhi saw when he renounced political leadership a few years ago on the ground that his influence was keeping the younger party from office and was in effect the use of power against them. This principle of Jesus is carried to its conclusion in his attitude toward offenders against society. Toward them he rejects completely the principle of retribution and relies upon their response to the desire of goodwill to change their lives. The practice and results of modern penology show the worth of this approach, show also how a basic ethical quality in the religion of Jesus can be developed to serve the needs of a modern situation in conjunction with the methods of science, which it needs to make it contemporaneously effective.

This principle of goodwill instead of power also governs Jesus' teaching concerning the relation of God to man; there is thus a cosmic reach to it. Herein is the bond of unity between the relations of men and their relation to God which makes an ethical religion. The absolute monarchical deity does not appear in the Gospels and all later revivals of him in the name of Jesus are cruel misrepresentations. The supreme power in the universe for Jesus is the power of goodwill.

It is because Jesus rejects power altogether, conjoined with the fact that he similarly rejects greed, that the development of his religion would lead the modern world away from war, not because of anything that he said or did about the use of force. Always in civilization the imperialistic and acquisitive principle appear together. The empires built on military power used it to collect tribute. Those built on the power of money and its right to interest use military means to hold their possessions. The modern empire of money relies upon force because it is built upon economic power, not upon goodwill working itself out in economic justice. What is won by power must be held by power. Therefore the acquisitive society is afraid to give up its armies and navies and unable to humanize and abolish its police and its prisons. It is caught in the net of its own making. Needing less war it yet will not abolish the concentrated wealth that occasions the new demand for the preparedness that inevitably leads to war. With a growing ideal of peace, it will not pay the price of it by abandoning its method of getting and distributing wealth. It finds itself continuously at war within itself because its basic process of competition sets the successful over against the losers. Its desire for democracy fails because while it seeks to substitute the process of reason for that of power in politics it still trusts to power in the economic world. Therefore with one hand we write peace treaties and with the other build a navy, manufacture bombing planes and poison gas, organize industrial preparedness. Peacemakers we would be, war makers we are because the works by which man lives, which have always been the ways of peace that men have left to go to war, are now the ways of war.

It is in its complete rejection of imperialism and acquisitiveness that the ethic of Jesus appears most impossible, because the organized ways of man have so long been actuated by power and greed. It is at these points that his sayings are either relegated to the *ad interim* position or proclaimed as revolutionary. Yet in their demand for a change of direction for organized human life there speaks the voice of the continuous moral aspiration of man, of the nobler side of his experience on this planet. This said Jesus, like the prophets before him, is also the voice of an inexorably ethical God. It is also the present dire need of the race. What chance has the acquisitive society to cure its sickness unless it can exorcise the power and the greed which are its causes. This time it is not a nationalistic or racial culture whose survival is at stake. Because industrialism is becoming world-wide and the machine universally used, what is in the balance is the survival of the race. Unless man can give up acquisitiveness and the desire to dominate the life of others he cannot endure. If a capitalist league of nations should be able to keep its members from poisoning each other wholesale, how will it then subdue the ensuing revolt of the subject nations and classes?

The cataclysmic class conflict on a world scale is no mere dogma, nor is it inevitable. But it is only avoidable by changing the dominant principles in the organization of capitalistic industrialism. This is precisely what is required by the development of the religion of Jesus. It points men toward the reorganization of life continuously around goodwill instead of power, for the pursuit of ethical development not material satisfactions. It urges them on to solidarity and equality, toward a world community of persons. Surely this is no cheap and easy way of salvation. It can be realized only if modern man repents and changes his ways. Otherwise the cycle school of history is justified and man goes once again out into the desert.

But if now we can broaden into a highway that search for justice and fellowship which has been heretofore only the trail of a few, then modern man may acquire a sense of creative process in his affairs and in the universe in which he shares because he has so chosen. Then cultural evolution may become one with ethical and spiritual development instead of the separate, divergent, and conflicting things that they always are in a civilization built on power and animated by greed.

It is this capacity of the religion of Jesus to urge life away from the evils that now mutilate and destroy it and forward into some organic unity, combined with the fact that it not only leaves room for but depends upon the experimental method, that constitutes its challenge to the scientific spirit. If those who are actuated by that spirit take nothing but a negative or indifferent attitude toward the ethical struggle because of the manifest deficiencies of organized religion, then science will more and more be prostituted to Mammon and so be made the means for the destruction of civilization. In view of the way in which science is now being used and limited in the search for profit it is nothing but a rationalization for current writers to assume that big business will develop its disinterestedness and make it the servant of society.

For the men of science as for the men of religion there is required a conscious choice of direction if either pursuit is to do anything other than make more certain the doom of mankind. To trust the money-makers to bring the good life to the world is just like trusting the medicine men—ancient or modern. There is no easy, indirect, or automatic salvation for man. Always there is the necessity for desperate struggle and for sacrifice. The road to life is the road through death. If the disinterestedness of science is to continue vital in the sense in which it is necessary, namely as intellectual objectivity, it will have to take sides in the human struggle. Otherwise it becomes merely the servant of the makers of empire, the rulers of the world. In the moral realm disinterestedness, in the sense of the neutrality of an onlooker enjoying the satisfaction of his curiosity, is not an admirable attitude. It is for those who feel themselves to be of the scientific enlightenment to make their choice. Which side of life are they on—the possessive or the creative, the destructive or the vitalizing? Are they aiding to strengthen and develop man the exploiter and killer or man the coöperator and creator? Are they content that the race should fight like wolves for their food when it is scarce, or crowd their feet into the trough like hogs when it is abundant? Or do they desire life to become an intelligently controlled process for mutual development? Are they satisfied with the standardized conformity on the surface of life that the machine controlled by the money-makers is now producing? Or will they seek the underlying unity of a common aspiration and a common goal, to be mutually achieved in serving and sharing?

If the farther goal is theirs, then the question is whether there is power in the cosmos to stimulate and respond to man's moral effort as its physical energy answers to his need. Is the nature of the universe such that it can only respond to man's practical needs, can but aid him to achieve an instrumental unity on the surface of life which enables the disrupting forces underneath to work more

[170]

effectively? At this point the religion of Jesus urges experimental development. For this purpose it makes available two sources of power, that which comes from the push of the movement in the life of man which it represents and that which belongs to the ideal that it upholds. This capacity it shares with other social movements particularly with the idealistic forms of socialism.

In addition the religion of Jesus assumes that there is available moral power in the universe beyond the strivings of man and his desires. This assumption it shares with other religions. But Jesus puts it in personal terms. He trusts the goodness of the Heavenly Father as science trusts the intelligibility and orderliness of the universe. Also he differs from ecclesiastical religion in declaring the power of God to be available only on ethical terms and for ethical ends. He does not offer to deliver it. He tells men to seek and they shall find. Whether it is personally realizable is obviously a matter of experimental test. If there are those to whom that test yields nothing, it is not thereby proved that nothing is available, any more than the validity of the scientific method is discredited because there are some to whom it does not bring any revelation.

On the whole the test is yet to be made. It is not that Christianity has not been tried, it is that the religion of Jesus has not been developed. The new realization of its ethical values brought about by the scientific method in religion brings a day of judgment to the churches. When men write about the decline of religion, it is ecclesiastical religion they are talking about. The world is still full of religion of many kinds. The question is what kinds are to survive. If life continues to be organized as the struggle of the greedy for power, then whatever forms of religion continue will be either a sanction for the winners or solace for the losers. For a few the alternative may be a bleak trust in cosmic intelligence. But this again is powerless to do more than help man endure a disintegrating social order and the tragic mystery of life.

The chief value of the religion of Jesus, now and always, is that it challenges man to develop his religion in and by changing his life. It does not ask him to merely repeat the experience of the past, not even that of Jesus, but to learn from it and then to enlarge it in the direction of more abundant living for all. It does not ask him to submit to any authority except that of experience and ideals. It does not say that Jesus' view of God or man is final or complete. It does not want him to use or respect the name of Jesus on any other ground than what he represents in human life and brings to it. Obviously his ethical values need to be tested and developed by the methodology of science. But his religion does supply the qualities in which science is deficient and in a manner congenial to it. There is no possibility of either saving civilization alone, because science by itself lacks drive and goal, while the religion of Jesus remains without practical form and content. But together they could keep modern man from rewriting the disastrous story of the ages.

CHAPTER IV

Is It Too Late?

1. RELIGION AND SOCIAL CHANGE

OF necessity the basic institutions of society—its government, religion, and economic organization—change gradually and slowly, no matter how suddenly their control may be transferred. The determining events usually happen with their nature and consequences unperceived save for a few people of vision who cry against them in vain, as when the United States took Hawaii and started on a career of imperialism. Then, when the outcome is unavoidable, men speak of destiny, fate, or providence to cover their own inadequacy from themselves. The inevitability of events is mostly an illusion. Most of the wrong courses in history were taken not because men chose wrongly but because they did not know they were choosing.

It is necessary, therefore, to ask whether American Protestantism has already unconsciously chosen its future course. Have events already determined its direction beyond our power of change, even though we understand their meaning? Is the choice really before us or is it too late? Is the weight of ecclesiastical tradition, much of it unbroken by the Reformation, so heavy upon our churches that they are not free to develop the ethical values in the religion of Jesus? Have our denominations given such hostages to the world in their great institutional projects that they are unable to resist its demands for support against impending changes in government and economic organization?

If the present interest in theology and worship is, as some of its advocates announce, a turning away from the social gospel and its call for an ethical religion then, of course, the die is cast and Protestantism becomes only a cheaper edition of Rome. In that case the recognition of the difference between the ethic of Jesus and the practice of the churches is only an intellectual substitute for action, the absorption in beauty of worship is a sign of decadence, the interest in the problem of God is mere indulgence in metaphysics and not a realization of human inadequacy for the task that lies ahead of us in getting rid of the evil that is in man and the world. Also the assertion of the freedom of the pulpit is but a compensating gesture against a control that is already made secure.

To the determinists this is the inevitable course of events, laid out by the inexorable dependence of the institutions of religion upon the rest of the social order. For them it is clear that an unethical society cannot and will not support an ethical religion, and equally clear that Western Christianity has not the power to transform an unethical society. Protestantism, they point out, has let economic activity remain so long outside the control of religion that it is now too late to establish spiritual sovereignty in that domain. Also it has now acquired such large property interests that it cannot rebel against the economic order no matter how unrighteous it may be, nor resist the state that protects it. Supported by it, institutional religion must either give it support in turn or perish.

While men may commit suicide, institutions do not. So the Orthodox Greek Church in Russia found it necessary to proclaim loyalty to the Soviet government.

This diagnosis and forecast raises and perhaps begs a larger question. Can a social order constructively change itself? As old age comes can it revitalize itself? Or like the individual must it face dissolution? In either case what is the rôle of religion? If the cycle philosophy of history is true and Western civilization is on the down curve, then organized religion has only one part to play. Its institutions decay with the rest of the social order of which they are a part, and its function is purely pastoral. It provides consolation for those who are aware of the sickness of society, as the philosophy of the Stoics consoled the nobler spirits of Rome in the days of its decline.

That senility is inevitable for races and their civilizations is however by no means proved. Some of the oldest are now showing signs of new vitality. New life is stirring in India and China. Awakened by the impact of the West, it manifestly has something to contribute to the world of the future, which can only be made by pooling all the resources of mankind. History will not repeat the story of the rise and fall of nations, the growth and decline of cultures. That has now been transposed to the world scale. From the impetus of industrialism and the scientific method mankind now develops common cultural characteristics. This means that while the diseases of civilization are at work everywhere, the vital resources of the race are now for the first time able to be joined against them. Man is becoming conscious of himself as a species, and is beginning to acquire the capacity to direct intelligently the whole range of his activities upon this planet.

For the first time man has within his reach the possibility of ending the historic cycle of the rise and decay of civilizations. Two forces in modern life are operating to fuse his separate cultures into a world order—the new knowledge and the new people. The new knowledge that comes through science brings more than new tools for common use. It gives the races awareness of each other and their past experience, of their common stake in the problems of life and the means for the control of destiny. It offers man the mastery of himself as well as of nature. It enables him to provide the necessary conditions for the establishment and continuance of a world order: the use of the machine and the resources upon which it depends under common plans to directly secure human well-being; the limitation of reproduction so that maximum development can be secured; the constant critical revaluation of institutions, standards, and values. The new people are the masses from the dark places at the bottom of society now being pushed up into enlightenment and power by the completion of the industrial revolution and the spread of education. They constitute vital resources of unbounded capacity. With the leadership of the men of science they can build a world which is beyond the reach of the money-makers and the seekers for power.

For mankind as a whole it is dawn, not the twilight that has fallen upon the dominant states of Europe whose shadow has already touched their vigorous successor upon this continent. The question of whether it is too late for this nation to enter that new day is the question of whether it is too late for it to abandon the ways of power and greed it inherited and then enlarged. Can it abandon its aggressiveness—both brutal and benevolent—and become a coöperating partner in a world order? Can it renounce its self-righteousness, lose its Messianic consciousness, and learn from other races? Can it revise the economic procedure by which it uses other nations to its advantage and keeps the people at the bottom of society—here and elsewhere—from developing? The religion which has proclaimed the ideal of a world order, which in the advanced sector of its missionary movement has been willing to fuse in joint search and effort with similar elements in other faiths, is now faced with the question of its capacity to demand and enable the necessary changes of spirit and purpose in our government and economic organization.

Here we meet the question raised in several of his writings by Coe, particularly in his recent work, *The Motives of Men.* He points out that the process of renewal for institutions as for persons is the constant critical revaluation of themselves and their works. Herein for them is the secret of an eternal youth that is unattainable for individual existence. But to be operative it requires repentance and change of ways. How then can institutions be led to repentance so that social change may occur by constant renewing instead of by decay or revolution? This is what religion has to discover. Science can aid in finding the process but it cannot motivate it. And unless it is carried on there is no escaping Spengler's conclusion. If this nation will turn aside from the path of empire and take up the trail that leads to a coöperative world order it can escape the destiny of the great powers that preceded it. Otherwise its fate is written.

It is at this point that the Marxians narrow and sharpen the issue for us. They are not despondent about the future of industrial civilization. They see it moving on to the world stage, but changed in form and nature, so that it brings new life to man. They look to the masses at the bottom of society to accomplish its renewal. The triumph of the working class, its seizure of the state and of economic control will inaugurate the coöperative commonwealth and so bring in a new day for humanity. For all thoroughgoing Marxians, the rôle of religion is to obstruct this change. It is a middle class institution whose function is to strengthen the *bourgeoisie* and to seduce the masses with false promises and illusions. Consequently it is to be fought as an agent and source of the counter revolution. It is to be destroyed with the classes. A classless society will not need it. Therein it will be replaced by science as the sufficient guide of man.

The logic is strong, indeed impeccable if the premise is sound. The question is do the facts support it. What is the function of religion in relation to social change? At a glance it is clear that its behavior is not simple, nor always consistent or unified. To say that religion is made by man upon the earth and not revealed from the heavens, that it is one of the institutions of society and consequently dependent upon the others, does not end the story. Like man himself, it is both created and creating, a product of society and a vital force affecting all social relations. It affects social change in two exactly opposite ways. It conserves and it alters; it is reactionary and it is revolutionary. It is reactionary because it puts the most powerful emotional sanctions and the highest justifications around established ways of doing things, because men's final justification of their acts is to insist that they are the ways of God. Were not the Kaiser and Woodrow Wilson equally sure of that? Religion is revolutionary because it directs attention to the ideal as a standard of criticism and a goal for endeavor. The difference in the social value of religions lies in the varying proportion of these two functions. That determines also the extent to which a religion becomes the tool and strength of a powerful, possessing class.

The variation in function also expresses the difference between religion as institution and as spirit. As institution, religion is tied in with the other institutions of the time. Therefore its dominant institutional influence and weight is against change, and the task of the minority who want social transformation is also to alter the institutions of religion. Therefore the measure of the capacity of organized religion to influence social transformation is its capacity to change itself—to abandon its outworn doctrines and forms, to separate itself from emoluments that perpetuate injustice.

When change impends or is in process, institutional religion provides security for the powerful and comfortable, while to the weak and distressed it offers the compensations of another world. Should they resist the mighty it will not offer them sanction any more than Luther did to the peasants. Then as an institution it will take the side of the established order.

It is only religion as spirit that offers inspiration to rebels, sometimes through minorities within the institution like that of the Poor Preachers in England who marched with the revolting peasants and were hung with them. It is a new religion not an old one—though it may be a break from the existing form reviving the spirit which the institution has almost strangled—that inspires revolutionary movements. It rises with them and strengthens their emotional force by putting the vision of the ideal behind the immediate interests for which they contend. It is because it transcends the events it judges and the forces it helps that religion in some form becomes the most powerful support of those accomplishing social change. It throws into the present situation the power of the eternal and so gives to those who are working and fighting the assurance of final victory. This pull of the ideal has never been entirely lost in the institutions of Christianity because of its heritage in the religion of Jesus and the prophets whom he fulfilled.

The transcendent function of religion also supplies a standard of measurement for the actual achievements of men and therefore merges into its critical capacity. It is by putting facts against possibilities that the modern world is convinced of sin and righteousness and judgment to come. Under the impulse of the scientific method organized religion has highly developed its critical faculty in recent years. Within the churches there is more revaluation going on than in any other social institution. The technic for the revaluation of life is being supplied to the young people. This marks our greatest gain. It is the contribution of the movement for religious education. At this point that movement becomes prophetic.

The social service movement in the churches has, somewhat unconsciously, been uniting the critical and transcendent aspects of religion, joining its conserving and changing functions. It has critically measured existing practices by the ideals of our religion, condemned some and approved others. It has cried aloud for serious changes in the nature and organization of society. So far it has not faced the question of what is required if those changes are to be accomplished without revolutionary procedure. It has assumed the possibility of evolutionary development and the efficiency of the educational method. This may prove to be as misleading an assumption in regard to industrialism as it was in the matter of war. It is suspiciously easy. The official social program of our churches depends upon the capacity of capitalistic industrialism to transform itself into a more just and efficient economic organization. But in place of critical revaluation and reconstruction it is now achieving further concentration of functionless ownership through holding companies. This means that under cover of minor reforms the basic evil is being increased. What then is the position of the social movement in religion and its attitude toward those who insist on going to the root of the matter?

2. THE CAPACITIES OF PROTESTANTISM

Thus our question narrows down to the capacities of Protestantism to influence economic change, to the rôle that it will play when the next stage of economic organization is being ushered in. The part of Rome may be regarded as settled. Its moral theology operates to abate the harshness of capitalistic industrialism and to support an interim position of compromise between capitalism and socialism. It is significant that it can get along with Mussolini but not with Stalin. If there is to be not merely a transfer of power but a real change in the nature of economic society in which the hitherto excluded masses take their place in the sun, then Rome plays a diminishing part. Its ability to survive as a refuge for distracted souls will be affected by the rate of the rise of a really scientific education and control of life, but more by the fact that its revenues will be cut. That fact determined its place in later England and will again decree its final place upon the world stage.

The future rôle of Protestantism is more of an open question. Its relation to the rise of capitalism has been sufficiently established. It was part of the same general movement; individualism appeared in religion as in economics. Its insistence that men can find God without a priest helped to make it the tool of men who wanted to find riches without regard to the welfare of others. That knowledge should by now be a part of the mental equipment of its preachers. That in its origin, nature, and present affiliations it is predominantly the religion of the middle class is sufficiently obvious. Its recurrent sects, arising in part as religions of the poor, have gone an unvarying way of transformation into denominations of the comfortable. They retain a fringe of the dependent poor, who both inherit and acquire their membership. The latter is done mostly for the loaves and the fishes, the former happens without any such connection between the program of the denominations and the economic need of this group as attended their early days. They are businesslike institutions, managed by business men—lay and clerical. Such ministers as are recruited from the ranks of the poor—and their number grows less—almost invariably acquire the psychology and ethics of the well-to-do.

This connection with the rise of the *bourgeoisie* sets the tone and temper of Protestantism, perhaps also its limits. Institutionally it is tied in with the system of money-making as early Christianity became tied in with the Roman Empire, and for the same reason—to advance religion in the world. Now as then, the religion of the churches is gradually conditioned by the religion of the world, which is to-day the cult of money-making. Just as ecclesiastical Rome took on the pattern of conquering, ruling Rome, so has modern Protestantism taken over the ways and works of the trading, investing West. Its theology as well as its management shows the marks of the trader and the bookkeeper, just as that of earlier peoples bore the imprint of the hunter and the farmer. Its ethics also have confusedly mixed the concepts of profit and service. So it has furnished both justification and sanctification for the pursuit of money-making, proclaimed it well pleasing to God and beneficial to man.

Along with the increasing institutional dependence of what were once religions of the poor upon successful money-making—not so much in gifts for extension as in returns on investment for maintenance of activities—there has come another current. The tradition of the ethic of Jesus breaks out once again, not in authoritative but in evolutionary form. To-day as never before, thanks to modern biblical scholarship, the leaders of organized Christianity are aware that the West has never really accepted Jesus, that the religion of the churches is not his religion. In other days rebel sects like the Lollards, the Anabaptists, the Levellers, have had this awareness. But it was induced largely by their own economic need and therefore somewhat limited to that interest. It should be our gain that the present widespread consciousness of the ethical nature of the gospel is more objective and general.

The question is how far will the churches go in developing the ethic of Jesus. Carried through, it requires a thoroughgoing and continuous transformation of society. It does not stop at good works or reforms, which if they are only that are but another cult of the prosperous. It is an ethic of service and sacrifice, and it takes life in a different direction than the ethic of conquest and enjoyment. It offers renunciation by the privileged as the substitute for the class war. There is no other meaning to the cross in social development. But what teaching of renunciation is there in modern churches? Who wants it among the intellectuals? To be effective as a teaching it must needs be practiced institutionally by the churches. Where are they doing it?

The more powerful institutions become, even though they cultivate the spirit of service, the harder it is for them to renounce their power or wealth because they are kept from seeing their nature. And above all else the Protestant denominations have become great institutions. Moreover the tendency to federate and merge is likely to increase still further their institutional as against their vital characteristics. It would seem that the trend is toward putting one great powerful Protestant institution over against the Church of Rome. This tendency moves in the direction of conformity to the world. This is the peculiar dilemma of religious movements which set out to conquer the world. Like the fighting nations they tend to take on the characteristics of the vanquished, so that at the very points where they appear to win they often lose. The movement becomes an institution tied in with the structure of society, unable therefore to provide needed moral judgment and secure conviction of sin because of the injury that would result to itself. So in time self-interest prevents it from seeing the moral deficit in its own life. Our denominations as employers are in no position to pass moral judgment on other corporations. The practical program of social reform which puts the churches in coöperative relations with public institutions—particularly the government—results in silence concerning major matters for fear of imperiling coöperation in minor advances. The attempt to work out constructively with business men a Christian industrial order is likely to stop at justifying profit by service.

The unvarying path along which original Christianity and practically all of its sects have passed, from revolutionary challenge to the principalities and powers of this world to acceptance of its ways and works, emphasizes once again the difference between religion as spirit and as form. And since religion must have body as well as vital essence it raises once more the question of whether there is some inherent defect in institutional life so that the achievement of form must always mean the defeat of spirit. Is it then the social function of religion to keep the falling torch alight, to stimulate others to snatch it up and start afresh, to give those who make the race some sense of its continuity? Or can it find saving grace to overcome what L. P. Jacks once called the "original sin of state nature," to give both persons and institutions an ever larger measure of victory in the perpetual warfare between spirit and body? Such saving power can only be found in developing the capacity to perceive and eliminate the beginnings of institutional decay. Once more we face the necessity of religion joining hands with science in developing and making effective a constant process for the revaluation and reconstruction of life. Once more it is evident that if organized religion is to generate such saving power for the rest of society it must begin with its own institutional life.

The spirit of Protestantism is congenial to this effort. Its genius is more than protest, it is freedom to search for truth. Therefore it has been more subject to the rise of sects than Rome. Therefore its orthodoxies have been less permanent and powerful. Romanism cannot in the end accommodate itself to the scientific method with its continuing revision of both truth and the organization of life. Neither can Protestantism if it becomes self-centered, more interested in its own perpetuation than in the continual working out of salvation for the life of man. But if it can avert the menace of its growing institutionalism it has a chance to really work out the scientific principle in religion and make it effective for the saving of civilization.

This possibility is translated into concrete terms at the basic point of the need for economic reorganization. Here Protestantism is faced with the question of its relation to the professions, and their relation in turn to the next step in social organization. The upper fringe of the middle class that makes up the body of Protestant adherents is composed of the technically trained people who provide the community with its engineering, teaching, medical service, law, finance, and business management. Modernism is the attempt to adjust theology to the intellectual needs of that small section of them who do any thinking outside their professional fields. It is an adjustment to the demands of science not to the needs of the masses. Its left wing call themselves Humanists, but where is the evidence of their appreciation of the situation that the majority of the people are in as a result of the dehumanizing aspects of industrialism? If modernism is to really become an intellectual emancipation it must also become a moral force. It must try without ceasing to change the life of the world as well as the thinking of men. It must insist that the strong and not the weak bear the cost of change.

There is a real test of the ethical efficiency of liberal Protestantism in the attitude toward social change of those members of the professions—particularly the technicians of industry—who have been reared under its influence, many of them trained in universities it has founded and endowed. What is their position toward the changes that are necessary if the people at the bottom of society are to be developed? Do they understand the economic reorganization that is required? Are they willing to pay their share of the price of it? Or is their ideal of life formulated mostly in terms of income, social position, and philanthropy? How many of them stand for the support of the existing order? The attitude of the technicians of society is a key point in determining the manner of its transformation. Unless there are sufficient of them who see the need of change and are willing to embrace its discomforts we shall get the next stage in social development by the driving force of the needs of the masses, without intelligent planning; and it will come with the maximum of friction and waste.

This test of the ethical value of liberal Protestantism may be extended to cover all the intellectuals within its fold and the students under its influence. What is their attitude toward the necessity and possibility of a new social order? It cannot come to birth without passion, the only question is whether it is to be created by the blind passion of the undeveloped, the intelligent passion for truth and justice, or a commingling of both. But intellectuals as a class despise passion. They tend to become anemic. This natural tendency is increased by the extent to which the laboratory method engrosses students in the immediate and the particular. They are deprived of the emotional drive that comes from understanding the past in relation to the needs of the larger world about them and to the possibilities of the future. They tend to become content with mere information and to assume that facts are automatically capable of transforming the world. They get to be afraid of a purpose and to regard a conviction as dangerous. Discussion is their main and often their only activity. When they turn from talking to doing, they are too often content with next steps without any vision of a goal. Also their churches are more inclined to show them how to do things for others than how to join the needy in the common search for social justice.

The educated section of Protestantism is not without signs of futility. Even where it is engaged in a thorough search for truth, because it is too much divorced from the struggle for justice, it tends toward intellectualism. The movement for intellectual emancipation within religion is in danger of falling victim to the ancient fallacy that knowing is doing. It needs to remember that the increase of critical capacity is usually and naturally accompanied by a decline of activity or the desire for it. This is now said to be justified by the need to keep the critical faculties unclouded by the emotions inevitably aroused in trying to change life, and uncontaminated by the dangerous air of partisanship. Here is evidence in plenty that we cannot trust the increasing capacity for self-knowledge and self-criticism to accomplish unaided the transformation of life. Not to the wise is it given to bring mankind to rebirth. They may not even show us the way unless their wisdom is illuminated with the passion for humanity. The only escape from the futility of a process of knowledge which makes man less capable of renewing his life is a knowing that involves doing, and a doing that is consciously accompanied by knowing. Such unity of experience requires the welding force of a creative purpose that embraces the whole of existence and its possibilities—personal and social, temporal and timeless. This it is the function of religion to supply.

Such a purpose does not appear in the current revivals of the æsthetic and intellectual aspects of religion. They move in another direction. The desire for beauty in worship tends toward the restoration of magic and mystery—the reservation of the sacrament and the mass. It is accompanied by an attempt to turn the preacher into the priest, to cut off that direct access to God which the Protestant revolt opened up for every believer. This completes the process of substituting religion by proxy for personal initiative, possessive for creative faith, which began when some Protestant congregations got rich enough to pay preachers and choirs to do for them what they wanted done. The æsthetic cult belongs to the prosperous and the powerful, to those who would use the past to strengthen their hold on to-day not to build to-morrow.

It is the weakness also of the intellectual movement in Protestantism that it is apart from the life and needs of the common people. What creative touch has it upon the great mass of church members? They spoke through

Bryan and wrote the antievolution laws, shouted with Billy Sunday, paraded with the Klan and drew up the blacklists of the D. A. R. The attempt to find either a rational basis or an ethical expression for religion is for the few. Among the crowd, as one of them put it, "religion is for marryings and buryings." The ordinary course of their life is directed by the symbols of business and patriotism and the conventional moralities, which are provided by the movies and the tabloids. Their world is hidden from the intellectual who is moved by the illusion of words and the symbols of logic. Concerning both of them and their symbols it may be asked, what do they know of God who only these things know? If religion is reduced to an intellectual formula in order to prevent rationalism from accomplishing its destruction, it has only escaped death at the price of slavery to the enemy. It is then unable to give men comfort in the unavoidable tragedies of life, the control of its corrupting and destroying passions, or a creative purpose to achieve the good life. It leaves the cultured cold and futile, the masses sodden and inert, until the whirlwind drives them both they know not whither.

3. SOME ALTERNATIVE RELIGIONS

If a secondhand ritualism and a sterile intellectualism is all that Protestantism has to offer the modern world its position may be regarded as settled. It belongs to the order that is passing, not to that now coming to birth. It will be written down as a bridge by which men passed from the religion of revealed authority to that of the scientific age, from the faith of conquering empires to that of the world-wide coöperative commonwealth. For both the prosperous and the crowds there are now more powerful alternatives. For those who think there is the religion of science and the religion of communism. For the unthinking there is the religion of nationalism and the religion of prosperity. They constitute two opposing alliances, drawn together by inherent qualities as well as by mutual opposition to the enemy. Is either of these, alone or in conjunction with its allies, to become the dominant religion of the immediate future?

(a) SCIENCE

The religion of science is now the authoritative revelation for those who reject all revelation and deny all authority. It has become the Messiah for those who abhor all Messiahs. The essential reason for its power is that it brings to man, harassed by the uncertainties of his existence, a degree of certitude before unattainable. That certainty is undoubtedly more limited than the devotees of science are generally willing to admit, but within its area it is exact. For long enough it has held the intellectual world under its spell. Now the other approaches to an understanding of life are again being surveyed and science is on the way to share its dominion with philosophy. Also realists are now recognizing that the conquest of life is an art as well as a science, that it is moreover a desperate adventure in which man needs a high religion.

It is a habit of the religious to say that science is only method. In fact, it is both a method and a faith. Essentially it is faith in a method. That it is a method which involves faith has been generally overlooked, largely because of the power of Huxley's famous slogan about

[191]

following the facts. But the laboratory method involves also the making of hypotheses, which are always acts of faith. Testing them is a further venture of belief in possibilities. The religion of science then is more than a passion for truth—in the form of observable fact. It is also a passion for following the facts to their conclusion —in the verifiable generalizations of theoretical science and in the courses of action developed by applied science. This much of the religion of science has already been gladly and profitably accepted in religion and philosophy by those who cannot endure closed systems. The creative scientists are a common company with the seers and prophets, journeying in the same direction, on the same search.

The religion of science has suffered the common fate of having its faith reduced to superstition by many of its devotees at the same time that its zealots have turned it into dogma. For them facts have become a fetich, endowed with magic power to change life when only perceived. But as a matter of fact, the mere apprehension of facts is dynamic only when values are determined and in so far as they are accepted. The publication of facts about slavery gets somewhere because slavery is judged to be wrong—that is, antisocial. But when values are yet to be chosen the facts only provide a part of the necessary materials for judgment. Their power is only to challenge decision and they are effective only with the prophetic spirits who anticipate the general verdict by their insight into the ideal, or their capacity to project the line of past value judgments, or both. The essential difference between the facts of human life and those of the cosmos is in the differing quality of the judgments called for, particularly their emotional tone. This leads some strict scientists to declare the impossibility of any social science and to aver that the term human sciences is a misnomer.

Akin to the prevailing fetichlike trust in facts in our universities is the superstitious reverence for intelligence. This is the common error of the intellectual. It repeats to-day the fallacy that paralyzed so much of Greek philosophy—that knowledge is virtue. In reality knowledge is not even the road to virtue unless people know for what they want to use it and how. They must also be willing. The only sense in which the possession of intelligence can guarantee man the capacity to work out his salvation is when very much more is included in that term than the process of the mind and the practice of the scientific method.

It is by the familiar logical error of assuming that because the empirical method is an indispensable tool it is therefore the only device for the discovery of truth and the attainment of virtue that many of the devotees of science are managing to destroy its capacity for enabling them to serve their generation. They isolate it from its natural allies until it can make no effective attack upon the destructive evils of modern society. Then they themselves lose the power to use it. Because all generalizations are tentative and subject to revision they will make no hypothesis concerning possible improvements in human living. Thus one of our journals takes pride in the announcement that it will not make any generalization to the effect that the economically powerful are following their selfish interests, despite the fact that it has published study after study showing in particular cases the degree to which this is being done.

Along with this unwillingness to follow the facts when they lead toward social change goes a distrust and even a fear of purpose. It is the fashion of the moment in the dominant school of the social sciences to shun purpose as the plague. Students are indoctrinated with the idea that to seek facts for any given purpose is to ensure bias. But this follows only when facts are sought in order to prove a dogma. It does not happen when they are sought for a great human end. When the purpose is the removal of cancer the search for the facts is not imperiled because cancer is a recognizable evil. So is war, so is economic injustice. It is then just as scientific to seek facts that will enable the abolition of war and the elimination of economic injustice. How absurd to say it is scientific to have a purpose to improve nature but unscientific to have one to improve human nature. This absurdity occurs however only when we are dealing with collective humanity. It is social purpose that is suspect in academic halls. It is scientific to use psychology to improve the capacities of the individual—even his capacity to exploit his fellow by successfully advertising unnecessary goods but unscientific to use science for improving the collective organization of life.

So we are getting too many sociologists and economists to whom even reform is abhorrent. They are so afraid of wish fulfillments and desire projections that they not only rule Utopia out of the universe but reform off the program. The only desire left is the desire to be comfortable. But this then grows strong enough to choke the spirit of science and to reduce its method to the tool of the class that controls the comforts. Thus is science betrayed to its death. If its discoveries are not universally used it loses that desire for universally valid truth which is its vital essence. If any class is able to control its results it will before long limit its search to that which is useful to itself.

To such use of science for class purposes the cult of objectivity now lends itself. One seldom meets more dogmatic opinions on social questions or finds judgments more influenced by prejudice and class interest than among men trained in the natural sciences. Especially when they have been professionally used by high finance. The scholar is traditionally as dry as dust. His natural inhumanity is increased when he is given a special interest, as when chemists argue the humanity of chemical warfare. The cult of objectivity has spread considerable confusion about the nature of disinterestedness. As a matter of fact, the scientist does not have the kind of disinterestedness toward nature that we are urged to acquire toward war. He has the kind of concern with its possibilities that leads him to action. He is actively interested in their discovery or use. He is not sitting in the bleachers, he is in the game. He has taken sides with truth. So in the moral struggle does the scientific spirit take sides with goodness, to promote its discovery and development. In both cases disinterestedness operates to keep the method free from entanglements not to prevent the choice of ends. Those who dodge that choice in the name of disinterestedness merely let others choose for them. The supposed detachment with which they view the millions battling in the arena of life rests upon the comfort and safety of the seat provided by the imperial powers and is by so much prejudiced in their behalf.

The religion of science is now in as much danger as the

religion of the churches of becoming a cult of the comfortable. If it is to continue its impetus for the discovery of ways to remove the evils that threaten civilization scientific men will have to make a further choice of social values than that which they have already made in their passion for demonstrable truth. In our associated human living what corresponds to demonstrable truth in the natural sciences is right relations—that is relations that work, grow, and endure. As men discover these, they enlarge them into ends like freedom, justice, fraternity. These are not merely transcendent ideals, they are expanding values. Also they are the occasion of conflict, their realization being opposed by those who in their own behalf, or that of their group, choose more limited ends. In this conflict science can no more be disinterested and remain scientific than it can in the battle between knowledge and ignorance, truth and error, superstition and certainty. Science dare not be indifferent to the ends for which it is used, because if it is used for limited ends it ceases to be science and becomes only one of the instruments of special privilege. Or it may find itself being used for the destruction instead of the development of mankind. It cannot help man to the continuous critical revision of his personality and institutions unless it is directed to those ends whose attempted realization is demonstrated by experience to afford the largest possible amount of well-being to humanity.

It is the province of science to provide man with the most efficient technic for verifying his ends. But this of itself is not sufficient for his needs. Something more than perfection of process is needed. Integrity and precision in method is not enough to guarantee the ongoing of civilization or a satisfactory meaning to individual existence. There is needed also the capacity to choose the highest—that is the most social—ends when they appear, and to pursue them at any cost. If modern man is to save either his society or himself he must be willing to die if need be for his vision of the possibilities of life. For that he needs a religion with more passion and drive than that now offered in the name of science. He must be conscious of the ends worth seeking as well as the means by which they can be achieved. He must have power to pursue them at any cost to himself.

(b) COMMUNISM

Such a power belongs to Communism and such a consciousness it seeks to give the masses. It is a religion of action which in Russia has taken science and put it to work in such a unified scheme for the improvement of human living as the intellectuals elsewhere, proudly free from its passion for humanity and limited by the organization of industry for private profit, have been unable to organize. For two generations millions of toilers in Europe, educating themselves with scant help and plenty of opposition from the culture of the universities, have been turning away from the religion of the churches to the religion of Socialism. This new faith gave them their God and their heaven. It was lit with an apocalyptic hope, that essential condition of vitality for any religion. More than that, while the older faiths were being discounted by the realism of a day in which science colored all education this new faith gained power by putting science into the service of its apocalyptic hope. While the churches were grudgingly adjusting their doctrines and their education to the rigorous demands of the scientific method, the Socialists were trusting it wholeheartedly. It is in Socialism that we find the real religion of science. Here science is turned to the search for human improvement and the organization of human well-being, proclaimed a sufficient guide for life, and worshiped with an almost superstitious reverence.

And it is among the Communists, the militant wing of the Socialists, that we find the full development of the religious elements in that movement. While the older Socialism has like the older churches been forced to conform at points to the world, compelled by the limitations of political action and office holding in capitalist countries to moderate its program, gradualize its action and limit its hope, in Russia with a clean field before it Communism has developed into a new state religion. The fact that it has been checked of its revolutionary hope and compelled to modify its apocalypticism, that it is even now developing once again the inevitable sects to quarrel over doctrines, only emphasizes the greater fact that it lives and works by virtue of its faith.

That it has worked mightily is beyond question, whatever may be the difference of judgment concerning the value of its works. What has been wrought in the organization of life in Russia in the past decade is almost incredible. It stands as one of the greatest bits of human engineering ever achieved. And it was done against tremendous odds. One of the two essential reasons that it could be done is that behind it is one of the most powerful religions ever developed by man. This fact is obscured by the paradox that this religion has been developed by those who deny all religion. For a parallel to their organization and discipline one must turn to the Jesuits or the Ironsides. Their faith and fervor, their certainty of a new world is, as Dewey has said, like that of the early Christians.

The faith behind this movement is threefold. It finds its pull in an hypothesis concerning the future of human society which is saturated with perfectionism. It believes in the possibility of ending the exploitation of man by man, of achieving the solidarity of mankind, abolishing classes and eliminating race antagonisms, through the organization of the world-wide coöperative commonwealth based on equitable and mutual economic planning. These are common beliefs of Socialists, but the Communists believe more powerfully than the rest and their hope is more immediate. Along with the pull of the future, to which it links man in faith and effort, Communism unites an impulse from the past of man. Its push comes from the irresistible economic forces in which the Communist believes as powerfully as the Calvinist believes in Providence. In place of divine decrees he has the revelation of unfailing economic laws which operate on his side and guarantee final victory. He parallels his predestinarian forerunner whose faith he derides by insisting upon the dogma of economic determinism—which in its wider aspects he calls historic materialism—even while with sublime inconsistency he works miracles with the revolutionary will. Here, in the force making for an inevitable outcome of the human struggle, is found the God of those who proclaim the destruction of all Gods. Looking at the comparative results, who will undertake to say that he is not a more powerful deity than the one worshiped in our churches?

The third article in the faith of the Communists concerns the mission of the proletariat. They are the chosen people appointed by economic law to lead mankind into the promised land of the coöperative commonwealth. Invincible they are, because of the power behind them and the destiny in front of them. Do not their sufferings fit them for the task? Thus the Messianic hope has become communized. The millions having done with the false saviors are now to save themselves, such of the intellectuals as will work with them, and the future of mankind. This they will do by foregoing whatever present satisfactions are necessary to be given up—including life itself, in order that all of the next generation may have access to whatever means of development the universe provides. This is the immortal hope of the Communists. It links the children of this brief day to a glorious and unending future of development for mankind.

The Communist assertion of the necessity of violence to inaugurate the new day for humanity which, along with its corollary of dictatorship, is the dogma that distinguishes and separates them from the parliamentary Socialists, is rather a deduction than a belief. They reason that violence and dictatorship are inevitable because of the certain refusal of the privileged to permit or abide by a parliamentary revolution. Thus, like the more rational of our own militarists, they generate a moral preparedness that requires physical expression and so do their bit to make their forecast come true.

It is obviously at this point of reliance upon force to overcome opposition that the religion of Communism takes the opposite road to that on which the religion of Jesus would lead mankind, though no different from that which the religion of the churches has to take when it allies itself with a professedly democratic state that intends to maintain itself by force. This was clearly demonstrated by our experience in the World War and the resultant repression of economic heresy. At this point the religion of Jesus is not only opposite to the religion of Communism but also to that of any state which seeks the welfare of mankind by the exercise of power. The patriots of such states have no ground in logic or ethics for denouncing the Communists for reliance upon force. If that aspect of the Communist program compels those who have taken up the religion of Jesus to regard it as a menace to mankind, they need also to ask themselves how it is related to the economic imperialism long practiced by the European powers and now being developed in the name of democracy by our own nation. They need to inquire how the Communist program can be avoided except by ending, before the point of revolution is reached, the use of force by other states to maintain functionless and antisocial property rights, and by hastening such a distribution of privilege that the masses can come to development without the waste of physical conflict.

The religion of Communism is also opposite to that of Jesus at the point of man's relation to the cosmos. Communism denies any cosmic help to man and regards any trust in it as superstitious faith. Its view of nature is exactly that of the acquisitive society against which it revolts—that the cosmos exists to be used by man. Those aspects of it which are neither usable nor understandable are to be fatalistically accepted. Vigorously denying all gods as it does, rejecting them as a hindrance to man's development, when Communism cannot avoid yielding to the universal god hunger and turning economic law and science into deities, it recognizes them as human creations.

It is the cosmic God the Communists deny. It is the God of superstitious magic, of metaphysical theology whom they cast out. The ethical God of Jesus and the prophets they neither know nor understand. Nor do they wish to.

What kind of ethical passion and conduct, what sort of social relations will result from this attitude toward the cosmos will be manifest when a generation which has been educated under this system, without the stimulus of a revolutionary hope, comes to power. Then we shall not need to spend time arguing whether man no longer needs that part of his nature and history in and through which he has reached out after some connection with the infinite, or whether what he requires is to have it transposed into modern terms. What is clear is that Communism stripped of its dogmatic glorification and use of force—in common with Socialism—gives us the religion of humanity. It is doing in action what Comte failed to do with theory. Here is the real religious Humanism, and it raises infinitely harder questions for both the religion of the churches and that of Jesus than the denatured variety that is being talked about here in a vacuum. Can the churches match the Communists in capacity for sacrifice? Do those who advocate the religion of Jesus produce as thoroughgoing and effective a program for the emancipation and education of the people at the bottom? These are the questions that will be asked by the masses and the intelligent alike when they awake from their bondage to our business civilization and go on the march once more to find a fairer habitation for the human spirit.

It is not impossible that the impact of science and of Communism upon the religious life of man will be felt more fully in the East than in the West. It is quite possible that the universal religion which the scientific movement and the movement for the elevation of the masses make possible will appear in Asia the ancient home of religion rather than in Europe or its cultural offshoots. It is significant that the Communist faith gets into action in Russia, where East and West meet, in blood, tradition, and culture. In these United States neither the religious aspects of Communism nor those of science carry any weight. There is no widespread desire for liberty, equality, fraternity, or justice. The dominant appetite is for comforts. The passion for truth—which is the vital essence of science —commands only a minute fraction of the population. Science itself is mostly harnessed to profit seeking business or put in bondage to purely utilitarian ends. Among us the claims of science to direct and of the common well-being to command life are overshadowed by the demands of two other forces—nationalism and prosperity. These hold most of the allegiance of the American people.

(c) NATIONALISM

It is a rhetorical fiction that Christianity is our religion. We do not even know what it is. Actually we have a trinity of religions—all mixed up together —the religion of the churches and synagogues, the religion of nationalism, and the religion of prosperity. The first person in this trinity is prosperity. From it the others take much of their form and substance. But in times of crisis nationalism takes command. In the days of war which of the churches, how many of their preachers or members, dare refuse its mandates? Now in times of peace it continuously extends its dominion over the individual conscience and asserts its authority against the claims of religion and morality. It puts a compulsory service of flag worship into the public schools from which sectarian religion has been debarred. In the churches it demands that the national flag be given precedence over the flag of the cross—the symbol of the universal need of mankind. It extends military training in our educational institutions and refuses to recognize the right of exemption to conscientious objectors. It makes the questioning of our form of government a heresy and punishes it with heavy sentences. Finally it refuses citizenship to those who will not submit to its orders to kill their fellow human beings.

Here is plainly the worship of the nationalistic state as God, even as it was in imperial Rome. Here too are the same demands upon the religious conscience for submission. Only now the Christian religion is not a missionary sect but powerful religious institutions all tied in with the life of the state and therefore much less inclined to withstand its demands—even though they destroy all that Protestantism has won in the freedom of private judgment.

Yet if the religion of nationalism—powerfully revived since the war in other countries than this—is not withstood, neither the religion of science nor that of humanity can grow. The right of private judgment, freedom for the critical intelligence and the sensitive conscience, are the conditions of a scientific as well as a religious order of life. The supremacy of the nationalistic state and its brutal separating passions is the death of science as well as of religion. Its suppression of the individual mind and spirit is the destruction of the creative capacity of human society. This will be found as true for Russia, for Italy, and the smaller states of the Balkan world, as it now is in the United States—all of them areas in which the war and its aftermath have revived or re-created the religion of nationalism with its atavistic passions, its machinery of torture and death.

It is the fact that nationalism, like imperialism, is to-day more economic than territorial or cultural which unites the religion of nationalism with the religion of prosperity until they are one flesh and one spirit. The broader aspect of this connection is the fact that the economic well-being of nations is to-day dependent upon competitive activity more than it is upon coöperative endeavor. In its narrower aspect this union is the control of the state by particular economic interests within the nation for their own advantage under the general illusion that this secures more goods and services for all. Thus on both counts—the control of international affairs by the stronger industrial nations in their own behalf and the direction of the policies of the state for the advantage of the stronger economic groupings within its borders—the religion of nationalism is used to put the powerful emotional values of patriotism and militarism behind the pursuit and practices of prosperity.

So the marine who has been brought to some Latin American country by the inevitable outcome of tortuous policies developed in pursuit of private gain dies in its jungle in defense of the interests of his country. So the citizen regrets but emotionally justifies his death, and if he is intelligent enough to appraise the policies that led to it is likely to rationalize them as necessary to the prosperity of both countries involved. The flag which he salutes and at whose mention in song he must stand to his feet represents to him not quite the same thing it did to his father. To-day it is not so much the symbol of freedom as of riches and power. It thrills him not by waving a welcome to the oppressed but by reminding him that he belongs to the most prosperous nation on earth. For the true militarist, of course, Mammon is too gross a god to worship. To secure the allegiance of the real fighting man, the money god must conceal himself in the shining armor of Mars and obscure his features by the illusion arising from the memory of all the heroes of the past who fought for freedom and for justice, for the poor and the oppressed. To get decent men to do the butcher work of the religion of prosperity by the modern methods of mass murder all the arts of romanticism, all the delusions of propaganda, must be employed.

(d) PROSPERITY

Similarly the religion of prosperity uses the religion of the churches for its own ends and brings even the spiritual desires of man into captivity to his appetites. For how many generations has it been widely declared in the churches and synagogues where the prosperous worship that the gaining of material prosperity is a sign of the favor of God? Always provided that a certain portion of the gain is turned to the support of religion and the relief of human suffering and ignorance and no questions asked! Thus the God of revealed religion becomes the God of prosperity. In a wider and more useful aspect this has always been true. Following an ancient practice, which long had more meaning, we are still officially called to give thanks to our God for our harvest—and a good many other things. So it has been quite natural for the prosperous to identify the pursuit and ownership of property with the will and favor of God. Years ago one of the magnates of the anthracite coal monopoly told our fathers that it was God in his wisdom who had given control of the natural resources of the land to the wise and religious men that they might be administered for the common well-being. To-day a representative of the new industrial South tells us that the men who are building its cotton mills have gone out on a spiritual adventure, being called thereto by their God. The consummation of this appropriation by the religion of prosperity of the God who was proclaimed an ethical deity in behalf of all mankind as long ago as the Hebrew prophets is the current widespread use of the term service to cover the pursuit of profit. Thus even the attempt to develop an ethical religion for the welfare of all is fenced in by the few for their own use.

If one wants evidence of the vitality of the religion of prosperity he has only to compare the fervor with which its ritual is recited in gatherings of the leading business men who are its priests and custodians with the more matter-of-fact observance of the ritual of synagogues and churches. Or he may compare the attention its devotees give to its scripture—the financial pages of the newspaper —with their interest in Bible or Torah. It has two great commandments which paraphrase those that sum up the obligations their religion imposes on both Jews and Christians—Thou shalt love the making of money with all thy heart and mind and soul and strength; and thou shalt love thy neighbor—enough to make a profit off him. Which form of these commandments—the original or the paraphrase—has more authority with our government, in both home and foreign policy?

The chief sign of the power of any religion is what men will give up for it. In the decade since the war the American people have given up in behalf of their prosperity a good deal of that which they before professed to value most. They loved freedom and boasted of their liberty enlightening the world. Now they steadily whittle down their constitutional guarantees of free speech, press, and assembly in the suppression of those who question the religion of prosperity. They welcomed the oppressed, now they keep them out; they are too dangerous to income or to the government that protects it. By their remoteness from the quarrels of the old world this people had developed a kindly spirit and their religion had inculcated a sympathy which had registered itself in a progressive attempt to remove some of the heavier burdens of the toilers. Now they refuse to pass an amendment to the constitution abolishing child labor. The argument that triumphs is that it will interfere with prosperity. In place of his own organization they offer the wage worker a company controlled union and a promise of higher wages to those who escape unemployment. To their colonial dependencies likewise they tender the hope of economic prosperity as something more valuable than their independence. Justice, freedom, sympathy—the highest values of life—we will give up for the sake of abundance of economic goods and services. Let every man search his own soul! What will he yield of his principles before he will diminish the comforts and conveniences that have become a part of his life?

The final sign of the power of the religion of prosperity is its ability to compel the offering of human sacrifice. In his formal religious life civilized man has long banished Moloch and it would be impossible to bring him back. But for nationalism and prosperity he will still pour the blood of the innocents upon the altars of Mars and Mammon. Of these two there can be no doubt which is the more powerful. We will not use gunboats and marines to annex territory but we do use them to protect financial interests. Already the industrial nations are agreeing that the toll of human life demanded by modern warfare is too heavy to pay. But for prosperity we sacrifice each year in this country more human lives in industrial accidents and diseases than we lost in a year of the World War. To this we add the devitalized children and the overworked mothers of the mill and mine towns, and on top of them the men who at fifty and earlier are flung out on the scrap heap without a thought because they can no longer keep up with the speed and stand the strain of efficiency production. This human sacrifice we ignorantly and selfishly put down as the price of progress. This one fact alone is sufficient evidence of the nature of the religion of prosperity. The exaction of human sacrifice is the sign of a false faith. To do it for the sake of increasing material possessions and creature comforts, which can be enjoyed only for a time and even then are incapable of satisfying the deepest longings of human nature, is the behavior of fools.

The character of the religion of prosperity is further revealed by the nature of its god. It devotees worship not money but success in the making of money. William James, knowing that it was not worthy to be called a god, described the ruling deity of the American people as "that bitch goddess success." By spreading the illusion that the attainment of culture and the extension of religion depend upon successful money-making the religion of prosperity in time reduces culture to a means to profits and degrades the Great God himself to the service of a lesser deity. What is the attitude of the money-makers toward the energy of the universe before which not only the ignorant and superstitious, not alone the lovers of beauty, but also the makers of science have stood with awe and reverence? To the acquisitive society nature exists only to be used, its God is but the servant of man's comforts, the universe is only a power house of mechanical energy. With such an attitude toward nature and its God man becomes inevitably the despoiler of his world and the exploiter of his fellow.

To make this more certain the religion of prosperity has evolved a corresponding doctrine of man. It says two things concerning human nature. It believes that man is essentially and irredeemably selfish; that his chief function is the creation and satisfaction of economic needs. So it holds that he can be moved to significant endeavors only by an appeal to his acquisitiveness, by enlarging his tendency to exalt himself above his fellows and at their expense. It offers salvation to society by the expansion of selfish desires not their control. It views life in terms of economic wants and efforts. The American Committee on Economic Change, composed of distinguished representatives of the nation headed by the man who is now its president, puts the keynote of its voluminous report in this sentence: "The conclusion is that economically we have a boundless field before us, that there are new wants which will make way endlessly for newer wants as fast as they are satisfied." What a prospect for human existence! What an occupation for the heirs of the ages! Then all our scientific and industrial activity has no more meaning or purpose than that set forth for the sons of pioneers in an old saying of the rich Mississippi Valley: "To raise more corn, to feed more hogs, to buy more land, to raise more corn, to feed more hogs. . . ."

It matters not that the hogs become refined and like clean sties with pictures on the walls and books on the shelves. History is plain enough about the outcome of a civilization that puts the pursuit of comfort and luxury into the first place in human life. When that is made into a religion it is but the religion of destruction, and to enlist the aid of both science and God in its behalf is only to make the end more certain. This is the issue that hangs upon the choice of trends in our official religion and before it the current controversy over Humanism looks like dangerous fiddling. Unless a religion can arise that is vital enough to destroy the religion of prosperity which is even now capturing nationalism and enslaving science there is no future before the sons of men.

This alternative is world-wide. In the Far East and the Near East the coming of science and industrialism is breaking up the ancient faiths and destroying the old religions. In Russia the work is well-nigh accomplished. But everywhere the tides of nationalism and class antagonism are rising and threatening new conflicts, some of which have already opened. Under the impetus of the machine all peoples are becoming engrossed in the pursuit of economic goods. From the course of events portended by these omens trust in science and the machine are no more likely to save man than a similar blind faith in the processes of evolution saved him from the World War. Because we cannot go back to the days without the machine and before science it does not follow that by them we shall automatically find salvation either from the quick destruction of universal conflict or the slow degeneration that accompanies absorption in the material aspects of existence.

Suppose the nations subdue the present causes of conflict; that the machine and mass production become universal; that the socialist ideal proves workable and world-wide; production and distribution is organized under a planned economy to secure the maximum development of all human capacities. Does it mean that there will then be no clash of personal and sectional interests? Does it guarantee man against fatty degeneration of the spirit? How will he avoid the inertia of the well-being whose securing has been his development? To keep in training for the battle that knows no truce between his appetites and his ideals, the interest of himself or his group and that of society as a whole, man needs an educational process that will develop him as a creative and loyal member of society, that will enable him continually to revise his life and institutions. But how can such an education develop or survive without the stimulus and support of a religion that constantly holds before man the vision of an expanding ideal, and imbues him with the passion to seek it?

4. THE RELIGION OF TO-MORROW?

Such a religion is both the need and promise of the times. Man as species is now struggling into organic life, reaching out his mind and hands to make the Great Society. To accomplish this he must decide to order his life around commonly accepted values and ideals, otherwise such organization as the machine imposes on him will only give him more things to fight about and more deadly weapons with which to fight. The common pursuit of a universal social ideal, like the choice of the values which compose it, requires a religious faith and passion linked with all the verified experience and method that science makes available. This kind of religion unites mankind in common action against the common ills of life and for the increasing realization of all its possibilities. It leaves man to be as divided in his thinking about his relation to the cosmos as the further discovery of truth requires.

The connection of religion with the other social forces is that of both cause and effect. So in times of change a new religious development appears and works, as Protestantism arose in the breakup of the medieval world. But this time it must be more cause than effect. We cannot wait for a new religion after the event. The nature of the new world order required by the joint demands of the machine and the rising masses is such that it needs new faith to bring it to birth. A great hope and passion for humanity is an essential part of the process of social creativity which man must now achieve if he is to continue his course. Mankind has now reached such a stage of mutual awareness, of common knowledge of itself and its history, that what it now does must be done together. For good or ill, in religion as in economic activity and in all the rest of culture, it is a collective world. The process of the great historic religions cannot be repeated. A new religion cannot again be born in the loneliness of one soul and its vision. All we can get that way is limited sects like Christian Science. Because we have reached the point where intellectuals the world over think in common terms and symbols, what remains to be done in religious creation is the expression of the needs and hopes of the millions. Whatever else it is the religion of to-morrow will be the religion of the masses. It will record the impact of their upcoming to the light upon the spiritual vision and destiny of man.

It is equally obvious that the faith of the future will also register the impact of science upon the mind of man. These two forces will play the largest part in shaping it—science and the dark millions. And science will become religious not in casuistic adjustments to theology similar to those which theology has long been making to it, but by consciously putting itself into the service of the masses. It will then realize itself spiritually in a social program much more than it could in the necessary negative task of correcting man's traditional beliefs about the universe and exposing his superstitions.

These two forces will see to it, if the present liberal wing of organized religion does not, that the religion of to-morrow is ethical. It will be ethical because it is social, because it frankly recognizes where and how moral values are made by social experience and therefore assists man in that process instead of trying to confine him to the customs and conventions of the past or limit him by laws made in the interest of a class. Its development of ethical values will necessarily take the historic line pursued by Jesus because that is the course along which society moves toward increasingly organic life. It will pursue further that mutualism in which he correlated not only individuals but also persons and the social whole. So it will aid man to achieve the synthesis between individualism and socialism, between the fullest and freest development of personality and the creative ordering of the common life. It will develop into social policies Jesus' reliance upon goodwill instead of power—even the Communists admit that to be the ideal and regret force as a temporary necessity. No matter how long it takes, we shall move constantly in that direction if we move at all. It is the only open road. The well worn highway of force and power leads only to a dead end.

The faith of the future will find its central task in applying the ethical principles which Jesus represents to the conquest of the means of existence. That much it will owe to Marx and those who have followed him. Understanding from them the strategic part of the economic process in molding social institutions, ideas and ideals as well as in limiting the capacities of human development, it will avoid the perennial defeat which they have brought to man's spiritual longings by intelligently directing and controlling them in the interest of the other values of life.

It cannot help being man-centered but not in pride and egotism, only in the ethical sense, in the same sense in which an ethical God must be because the process of creating an ethical society is an absorbing end requiring service and sacrifice from both God and man, uniting them in an enlarging fellowship. Concerning the question of man's relation to the cosmos this religion will increasingly lean upon science but it will act in its own right in making the assumptions that have to be made concerning its nature. It will have to test experimentally the faith of Jesus concerning the personal goodness in and back of the universe, for only by trusting the cosmos far enough to plan and work for the future can it save man from the futility that follows increasing self-consciousness without action. It will aid him to the conquest of life by assuming its ethical meaning, and by putting ethical purpose into life instead of arguing about whether it is there. So it will not leave man lonely and defeated by the catastrophes and failures of existence. Where he can find no victory it will give him the assurance that, by allowing him room for an ethical struggle in which he can find both himself and his fellows—in all time and beyond it—through the creative effort to achieve a society, the universe has been friendly enough.

Thus by giving science and philosophy a social meaning and purpose the religion of to-morrow will unite man's thinking and action in some unity of experience. This coördination will give him the promise of victory in that old war on two fronts in which the spirit fights both the flesh and the world, because it will show him their relationships. The more he understands about the nature of the flesh and its connection with mind and spirit, about the history and meaning of the conventions that have arisen to govern it, the less power it will have to mutilate his existence, or to bring him into bondage.

5. OUR PART

The part that American Protestantism will play in relation to the future religious development of mankind is now in the balance. Despite its dominant tendency toward institutionalism it is not yet set in rigid form. The forces that will give it shape are still in flux, struggling against each other for the mastery. It has more dissenters than any other institution tolerates. Its sectarian divisions, which the older churches regard as its fatal weakness, are the sign of creative capacity and possible adjustment to religious developments elsewhere. Also they raise the possibility that it may become not merely another great church but one of the currents flowing into the religion of the new social order. This promise is held out also by the open-mindedness of its theology toward the religious aspirations and thinking of other forms of religion, an attitude that makes possible a fusing of life not a mere merger of organizations, a union that is dynamic not static. Of all existing forms of religion it gives most room in its left wing for the process of critical revaluation which holds the secret of how institutions can only save their lives by losing them.

If it can go through to the bitter end with its spirit of freedom and criticism, if it can also develop the ethical passion and power of the religion of Jesus in support of a social program based on an understanding of the processes of history and the nature of man and society, liberal Protestantism can become a revolutionary religious movement in the scientific sense of that term. This means a religion which never regards itself as fixed or final but is continually adapting itself to the needs and movements of life, always going on to perfection as the saints have ever done, and as the scientists and all institutions must do if they are to continue to live.

It is not yet too late for American Protestantism to become a creative religious force instead of that obstruction to the next step in human development which much of its heritage from the older forms of Christianity and much of its own attitude in the past toward the emancipation of the mind of man inclines it to be. But this course is only possible if it develops the religion of Jesus and that means at least as much of a change from twentieth century ecclesiastical Christianity as it did from first century traditional Judaism. The test question is its attitude toward the dark millions and their need. The issue with science may be regarded as settled despite the recent vociferousness of Fundamentalism. That was the dying shout of a lost cause.

What part they will choose to play in the greatest social drama of history in which millions of dark people the world over are coming to a place in the sun is the judgment test of the middle class of this country. If their religion follows the broader line of its long spiritual and social ancestry rather than the narrower ecclesiastical tradition immediately behind it, they may gain the power to take up the shock and lessen the waste of inevitable social change in a manner never before seen. They are politically powerful enough if they choose to do it to turn their country from its present tendency to become the center and support of world reaction by its defense of antisocial forms of property. They could lead it to play a significant part in shaping the Great Society by dedicating its resources and technical skill to a general plan for the common well-being of mankind. Failing this, their religion will become another cult of æsthetic or rationalistic escape from the discomforts and perils of revolutionary times. Instead of heralding and helping to bring to birth a new world, it will merely conduct the obsequies and console the mourners of the old order into whose grave it is soon itself to fall.

In estimating the outcome the present tendency toward church union is significant. If it means merely more organization of the same sort, its very weight will make change harder and its increased self-interest will render it more liable to give support to the imperialistic state and the forms of property which it protects. Just as significant is the present struggle between the intellectual, æsthetic, and ethical aspects of religion. The capacity of religion to serve either the scientific thinkers or the millions depends upon its ability to bring both its theology and its worship to bear directly upon the present behavior and future possibilities of man and his institutions. This means that the leaders of American Protestantism need to understand the nature and consequences of the choices that now lie before it.

But the choices that determine the fate of human institutions have not in the past been made consciously. Even when minorities break out to start new movements they usually go forth under some irresistible compulsion of mind and conscience without any certainty of whither they are bound. To-day we have a knowledge of the past that makes conscious choice possible but it is limited to a minority in whom the method of acquiring it has too often atrophied the capacity to act.

Also the decisions that determine the destiny of institutions and civilizations are always a graduated series. They are made upon the field of action under the pressure of present necessity. So the future course of American Protestantism, whether it is to be a force making for a social religion or merely another ecclesiastical organization, will be settled by certain concrete decisions of its leaders, denominational and interdenominational. For instance, if war comes again will the denominational and interdenominational authorities lend or refuse the support of their organizations? If the Supreme Court decides that in its requirements for citizenship the nation will not allow the right of private conscience in matters even of life and death, will the authorities of the Federal Council of Churches and the denominations offer and counsel resistance? Will they do this if the line is drawn only against the conscience of those who stand outside the official boundaries of religion? Will they stand as vigorously for the right of the workers to organize and to advocate change in our political and economic institutions as they stand for the freedom of religion and of the mind of the intellectual? Will they denounce and oppose even against their own vested interest, antisocial forms of property? It is at points like these that the future of organized religion is experimentally determined, that its decisions either put it into bondage to the other institutions of society or make it their emancipator by helping them also to decide immediate issues in the light of enduring values.

That there are tendencies in the American churches toward sacrificing ecclesiastical interests in behalf of wider social values will not be denied. But the probabilities of their becoming dominant are manifestly less than the possibilities. They have yet to feel the full weight of resisting tradition, they have yet to meet the full force of the opposing world. If capitalism proves incapable of being gradually transformed into a more efficient and ethical economic order the probability of Protestantism becoming an ethical religion is further dinimished, for from their beginnings the life of these two have been intertwined— in both action and reaction. But the incalculable element in any revolutionary struggle, as Trotsky the determinist— of all persons—has recently reminded us in the story of his life, is the reserves of personality. So it is in the undeveloped capacities of that minority in our churches who have the vision of an ethical religion, along with the desire to realize it, that the future of American Protestantism lies hidden.

For them it is never too late, because their function is not to seize power but always to remain a minority, never content to rest on any ground won, always pressing on to new frontiers. The work of their hands cannot come to nought. If not here then elsewhere the principles for which they stand, because they are indispensable to the ongoing of human institutions and the realization of personality, will animate the religion of the future.

GEN. THEO. SEMINARY
LIBRARY
NEW YORK

[221]

GEN. THEO. SEMINARY
LIBRARY
NEW YORK